Richard completed pupillage with 5 Paper Buildings in 2014, obtaining tenancy at the set and has continued to practice since. His practice encompasses a range of criminal matters, with a particular focus on fraud, money laundering and confiscation. Richard's practice often encompasses the use of expert witnesses and is regularly instructed to advise and represent individuals with mental health concerns.

Alongside publication of this book Richard presents a seminar series on the use of expert evidence in criminal trials, delivering presentations to both prosecution and defence practitioners on how to use and challenge expert evidence in criminal proceedings.

A Practical Guide to the Use of Expert Evidence in Criminal Cases

A Practical Guide to the Use of Expert Evidence in Criminal Cases

Richard Padley

Barrister, Inner Temple

Law Brief Publishing

Published 2023 by Law Brief Publishing, an imprint of Law Brief Publishing Ltd
30 The Parks
Minehead
Somerset
TA24 8BT

www.lawbriefpublishing.com

Paperback: 978-1-914608-50-6

PREFACE TO THE SECOND EDITION

It is a privilege to be able to write a second edition of this book. Since the first edition was released in 2020 the higher courts have continued to provide comment on both matters of procedure and substance relating to the use of expert evidence in criminal proceedings.

Matters relating to mental health continue to flood the courts. Since the first edition of the book was published the Sentencing Guidelines Council have released a guideline to assist practitioners understand the options available at the disposal stage of cases where mental health is an attributable factor to the subject matter of the case. A lot of work still needs to be done in recognising, understanding and applying factors of mental health at all stages of proceedings, from pre charge advice and charging decisions through to disposal. But it is getting there. Mental health remains an underfunded area and use of the criminal justice system should not be seen as the default position simply because funding is not provided to address the root cause of the issues.

This edition also includes a chapter on the use of experts to assist in cases involving the modern slavery defence. Over the past few years the Court of Appeal has found itself regularly having to deal with issues surrounding the NRM procedure and how this fits into the s45 defence. This is an area that will not go away and will continue to be discussed and debated in the higher courts for some years to come.

My continued thanks go to all those at 5 Paper Buildings who continue to offer me support, guidance, and with whom I've been able to discuss this book. Further thanks to Eleanor Fox, (former pupil at 5 Paper Buildings) and Ryan Evans (current pupil at 5 Paper Buildings, and my first pupil) for their help in researching this book. Any mistakes are of course my own.

And of course, my thanks to my wife and children, Kelly, Lily and Tom, for their continued support.

The law is believed to be correct as at 1st March 2023.

Richard Padley
5 Paper Buildings
1 March 2023

PREFACE TO THE FIRST EDITION

When I first started out in practice one of my earliest cases involved defending an individual charged with causing the unnecessary suffering of an animal. Whilst all of my work at that stage involved an excessively large number of hours in preparing for trial (matters I'd now consider relatively straightforward and not requiring such a level of preparation) this case certainly had a number of hours preparation that was closer to three figures than two. What made this case significant in terms of my preparation was that it involved the cross examination of two expert witnesses – in this case, both veterinarians. This was my first case involving expert evidence. It taught me the importance of preparation. Never had I ever read so much about feline immunodeficiency virus in my life (and I doubt I ever will again). But even now I suspect I would get a rather good score on Mastermind about the topic.

The case taught me about the importance of knowing the subject matter when having to go toe to toe with an expert witness in the courtroom. This can only be achieved through preparation. But reading about a subject that your opponent has spent their entire career studying and practicing, can remain a daunting prospect for even the most seasoned practitioner.

The aim of this book is to assist practitioners in preparation for tackling that challenge. The book seeks to assist practitioners in understanding how experts feature in the criminal justice system. Without an understanding of the role of the expert, or what the opposing sides expert will say, cross examination cannot be effective. With that in mind the book goes on to specifically deal with several areas of expertise to assist the practitioner get to grips with an expert's report from the first time it is read. It is a book that I hope is accessible to both the junior practitioner first starting out in the profession as well as the more seasoned practitioner looking to update and refresh their knowledge. It is aimed at both defence and prosecution practitioners, because knowing how the other side are likely to seek to undermine an expert's report is fundamental.

Despite the hours of preparation, and a challenging experience in cross examining two vets on the topic of feline immunodeficiency virus, I was not successful in that case. I was however to meet my lay client again, 18 months later, charged with terrorism offences. But that is a story for another book...

Many thanks to my chambers, 5 Paper Buildings, for giving me the opportunity to qualify and develop my career to date. My pupil supervisors, Dominic Lewis, Nicholas Fooks and Charlene Sumnall for getting me through my first few years of practice and continuing to act as a source of support. Also, to Dorian Robinson (pupil 2019-2020 at 5 Paper Buildings) for assisting me with the research and proof reading of this book (any mistakes are of course my own). Finally, to Kelly, Lily and Tom – whilst this acknowledgment won't replace the time I've spent working away from you all, perhaps it's a start.[1]

The law is believed to be correct as at the time of writing, 23 May 2020, excluding any temporary amendments to the law enacted as a result of the COVID-19 pandemic

Richard Padley
23 May 2020

[1] Or a holiday.

CONTENTS

INTRODUCTION

Experts hold a special place in the criminal justice system. Unlike ordinary witnesses of fact, they are not brought into proceedings because they happened to be at a particular place at a particular time. Instead it is because of what they know. What they know will have been built up over many years, in several different ways. It is the act of building up knowledge over many years of research, practice, and understanding that makes the individual an expert.

Why is all of this of such importance to criminal practitioners? An expert can give evidence not only on matters of fact, but also on what those facts mean and their significance. They can give 'opinion' evidence. Such is the importance and impact of expert evidence on a particular party's case, Judges will often remind juries of the need to see that part of the evidence in the context of all of the evidence in the case.

Recent cases have demonstrated that selecting the wrong individual as an expert can have a devastating effect on a case. Ensuring that the expert selected to assist your case is appropriately qualified should be at the forefront of all practitioners' minds. Practitioners should be more aware now of the need to get the right expert involved as early as possible, and the consequences of failing to do so.

The aim of this book is to act as a guide for practitioners in understanding how expert evidence can be used to develop a case, as well as highlighting the principles that underpin the use of expert evidence in the criminal courts. It focuses on a number of areas of expertise that many practitioners will have come across during their career and offering an insight into how to understand this evidence and how the courts have considered these areas.

CHAPTER ONE

AN INTRODUCTION TO EXPERT EVIDENCE

> *" ....It is true that the witness who is called upon to give evidence founded on a comparison of handwritings must be peritus ; he must be skilled in doing so; but we cannot say that he must have become peritus in the way of his business or in any definite way.* ***The question is, is he peritus? Is he skilled? Has he an adequate knowledge?."***[1]

Over 125 years since the above comment was made in *Silverlock* expert evidence, its quality, its appropriateness, and its limitations remain of great debate within the criminal jurisdiction. The past few years have seen high profile cases highlight that not all individuals advanced as experts are necessarily as '*peritus*' as they believe themselves to be. Time used scrutinising and examining an expert's report, their background and qualification, can prove more fruitful than one may originally consider.

What is expert evidence?

Expert evidence is evidence of opinion falling outside the experience of a judge or jury. By contrast non-expert evidence goes to matters of fact. The oft quoted judgement of King CJ in the South Australian case of *R v Bonython* notes the distinction:

> *"whether the subject matter of the opinion is such that a person without instruction or experience in the area of knowledge or human experience would be able to form a sound judgment on the matter without the assistance of witnesses possessing special knowledge or experience in the area; and whether the subject matter of the opinion forms part of a body of knowledge or experience which is sufficiently organised or*

---

1 [1894] 2 QB 766 at 771

> *recognised to be accepted as a reliable body of such and a special acquaintance with it by the witness would render his opinion of assistance to the court."*[2]

The Court of Appeal observed in *R v Dlugosz and others*[3] that in considering the issue of whether the evidence sought to be adduced is expert evidence, and potentially admissible as such, the court must be satisfied that there is a sufficiently reliable scientific basis for the evidence to be admitted and tested before the jury. The untested views of an individual are unlikely to find favour before the criminal courts.

Areas of expertise that practitioners will have often come across involve elements of technical or forensic analysis. These can include:

- DNA evidence – to assess the likelihood that DNA found on an item of interest has come from a person of interest

- Psychiatric evidence – to assist establish an individual's mental state at a particular time of relevance

- Firearms evidence – in assessing whether a particular item falls within the definitions under the Firearms Act 1968

- Cell site evidence – to establish location and movement of a sim card

- Facial recognition – to assess the likelihood that a person shown on CCTV/photograph is the same as a person of interest

However expert evidence is not exclusively based around science or forensic analysis. Areas of expertise perhaps less routinely used have included:

---

2 R v Bonythön [1984] SASR 45

3 [2013] EWCA Crim 2

- Historical facts about Al-Qaeda – *Ahmed* [2011] EWCA Crim 184
- The political and economic situation in Russia – *Berezovsky v Hine* [2011] EWHC 1776 (Ch)

There are however areas where an expert should not stray. It is now well established that an expert cannot go to the question of whether or not an individual is truthful.[4] The question of whether a witness is truthful and reliable is a question for the trier of fact and not for the expert.

Additionally, whilst matters of foreign law can often be subject to expert evidence the law of England and Wales is not a proper subject for expert evidence since it falls within the competence of the court.

The evidence an expert gives should be based on admissible evidence, and it is incumbent on the advocate calling the expert to adduce the underlying admissible facts during the evidence.[5]

Who can be an expert?

An expert is an individual who has specialist knowledge in a particular subject area. That specialist knowledge can be gained through years of experience, whether in the pursuit of research and academic study, the practical application of the field of knowledge through work, or often a combination of both.

> *52. The next criterion is whether relevant expertise had been demonstrated. The old authorities talk of 'men of science' and much of the discussion about expertise revolves around recognised disciplines in science or medicine. Yet it is well recognised that it is possible to become an expert by practice and experience*[6].

4 R v C [2012] EWCA Crim 1478

5 R v Terence Turner [1975] QB 834

6 R v Brecani [2021] EWCA Crim 731 at para 52

As outlined in the above passage from *R v Brecani,* qualification as an expert can be gained through academic qualification or vocational practice and experience. Some areas of expertise are constantly changing and being updated, and consequently 'on the job' experience is essential. Very often experts will have a combination of both academic qualification and practical experience form which they can draw.

In selecting an appropriate expert, the interplay between their knowledge and expertise is a relevant consideration. Whist an expert is entitled to apply their knowledge to reach a conclusion by, for example, referring the academic papers of others in the field[7], that knowledge should be evaluated by the expert by reference to their practical day to day experience[8]. An individual who has a purely academic knowledge of a subject may certainly be described as an expert, but the opinion given by such an expert may well be given less weight with the court than that of a person with a combination of academic knowledge and experience[9]. That is not to say that academic training cannot engender appropriate experience in the right circumstances.

The importance of qualification was explored in the case of *Brecani*[10] when considering the admissibility of the 'conclusive grounds' decision in the assessment of whether an individual could be categorised as a 'modern day slave'. The Court of Appeal noted the following as part of their decision in ruling the evidence inadmissible:

> *53. In this case, and in respect of decisions by case workers assigned to the Competent Authority generally,* ***no information was available upon which it is possible to determine whether and in what area the case worker might be an expert.*** *Beyond an inference that decision making is approached via the comprehensive guidance to which we have referred and that there must be some training provided, case*

7 R v Abadom [1983] 1 WLR 126

8 R v Weller [2010] EWCA Crim 1085 at para 38

9 Ibid

10 [2021] EWCA Crim 731

workers in the Competent Authority are junior civil servants performing an administrative function which includes making reasonable grounds and conclusive grounds decisions. The guidance recognises that a decision of the Competent Authority might be disclosed in criminal proceedings but nowhere is there any suggestion that the decision maker might be called to give evidence, still less that in making the decision the case worker is acting as an expert and might give evidence in chief and be cross-examined in a criminal court as such.

54. In respectful disagreement with the Divisional Court in DPP v M we do not consider that case workers in the Competent Authority are experts in human trafficking or modern slavery (whether generally or in respect of specified countries) and for that fundamental reason cannot give opinion evidence in a trial on the question whether an individual was trafficked or exploited. ***It is not sufficient to assume that because administrators are likely to gain experience in the type of decision-making, they routinely undertake that, simply by virtue of that fact, they can be treated as experts in criminal proceedings.*** *The position of these decision-makers is far removed, for example, from experts who produce reports into air crashes for the Air Accident Investigation Branch of the Department of Transport which are admissible in evidence in civil proceedings: see Rogers v Hoyle [2015] 1 QB 265 .* ***Moreover, none of the requirements of CrimPR 19, designed in part to ensure that the person giving evidence is an expert, understands he or she is acting as such and understands the obligations of an expert to the court, were complied with.***

In the above passage the Court of Appeal makes a number of important points. First, the requirement to comply with part 19 of the Criminal Procedure Rules. As set out in Chapter 2 Part 19 of the Criminal Procedure Rules provide the relevant provisions relating to expert evidence. Secondly, repetition of process does not make an expert. As was outlined in *Brecani* decision makers under the National Referral Mechanism follow guidance and perform an 'administrative function'. The act of performing an administrative role in line with guidance provided was insufficient to make an individual an expert in the area. But the Court did leave open the possibility to the admissibility of expert evidence in the area of modern slavery. The Court commented:

> *58. Mr Douglas-Jones appeared at the appellate level for the prosecution in DPP v M . At [45] the court noted that it was no part of his argument that expert evidence was never admissible on the question of trafficking and exploitation. He readily accepted before us that there can be circumstances in which a suitably qualified expert might be able to give evidence relevant to the questions that arise under the 2015 Act which are outside the knowledge of the jury, particularly to provide context of a cultural nature. That is clearly correct.* ***The evidence would have to be truly expert and not a vehicle to enable the expert to stray into the territory of the jury by expressing his or her personal opinion about whether an account is credible or inconsistencies immaterial.*** *As the present case vividly illustrates, the conclusion on whether the prosecution has disproved the section 45 defence will call for an assessment of all the relevant evidence which the jury is well-placed to make.* ***In the right case that evidence might include expert evidence of societal and contextual factors outside the ordinary experience of the jury.***

The developing area of the use of modern slavery experts is explored further at Chapter 10.

Challenging Expertise

Whilst many profess to have expertise, whether an individual truly does, and whether they hold said expertise in the area relevant to the matters in issue. It is an important principle that an expert can only give expert evidence in an area within their expertise. The case of *R v Alex Pabon*[11] started a string of cases in which this issue was brought to the fore.

[11] [2018] EWCA Crim 420

Alex Pabon

Alex Pabon was found guilty after trial of a single count of conspiracy to defraud, in respect of dishonestly rigging the London Interbank Offered Rate (LIBOR). During the trial the SFO relied upon an expert witness, Saul Rowe. Mr Rowe was also used in the retrial of two of Mr Pabon's co-defendants, Mr Stylianos Contogoulas and Mr Ryan Reich. During the retrial material was revealed to the prosecution and the defence undermining Mr Rowe's abilities to act as an expert in these proceedings – email correspondence was disclosed that another partner at Mr Rowe's firm had in fact produced parts of Mr Rowe's expert report, and text messages from Mr Rowe to others relating to matters on which he was giving evidence.

In summing up the matter to the jury HHJ Leonard QC highlighted the matter within the following passage:

> *"Despite that catalogue of experience, you may have formed a judgment that he knew very little about the duties of being an expert......he seems to have been perfectly content to sign a standard declaration in which he declared that he had read the Criminal Procedure Rules which govern his conduct as an expert, both before trial and in giving evidence, and the booklet on his duties of disclosure without doing anything really to familiarise himself with either of those documents.* ***It will be for you to judge whether he has in fact given expert opinion which falls outside his true expertise. Any expert is entitled to research a topic on which he is to give evidence and obtain the views of others, including work colleagues, about it to enhance his opinion, so long as he records where he went for that advice and so long as it is to enhance an expertise he already has, rather than to become an expert on a subject where he has no knowledge whatsoever.***[12]

12 As outlined in R v Pabon [2018] EWCA Crim 420 at para 52

The passage highlights several important matters:

1. It is for the jury to determine, upon hearing the evidence, how much weight to put on an expert's evidence.

2. Whilst an expert is entitled to update their knowledge of matters on which they are due to give evidence including by approaching third parties, those communications should be logged and reviewed for disclosure.

Evidently, and perhaps without needing to be stated, it is clearly undesirable for an expert witness to attempt to become an expert in an area they hold no previous expertise during the trial.

In considering what makes an expert the court went back to 1894 and the case of *Silverlock*[13] and the judgment of Chief Justice Killowen:

> " *....It is true that the witness who is called upon to give evidence founded on a comparison of handwritings must be peritus ; he must be skilled in doing so; but we cannot say that he must have become peritus in the way of his business or in any definite way. The question is, is he peritus? Is he skilled? Has he an adequate knowledge? Looking at the matter practically, if a witness is not skilled the judge will tell the jury to disregard his evidence. There is no decision which requires that the evidence of a man who is skilled in comparing handwriting, and who has formed a reliable opinion from past experience, should be excluded because his experience has not been gained in the way of his business......* "

As explored earlier in this chapter, and highlighted in the above passage, an individual can become an expert in a broad range of ways. As was noted by Bingham LJ in *R v Robb*[14] English law is "*characteristically pragmatic*"[15] in establishing expertise. This benefit of this broad approach

---

[13] [1894] 2 QB 766 at 771

[14] [1991] 93 Cr App R 161

[15] Ibid at 164

to characterising expertise allows the issue to be examined on a case-by-case basis taking into account the particular individual advanced as an expert and the particular issues in the case that are highlighted as requiring expert evidence.

Ultimately the Court of Appeal upheld the convictions in Pabon and others based on the relevance of the expert's evidence to the ultimate matter in issue at the trial – the expert didn't speak to the issue of dishonesty in respect of the Appellants' actions, and therefore could not have affected the safety of the convictions.

James Byrne and others [2021] EWCA Crim 107

Almost as soon as the *Pabon* case was ending issues surrounding a different expert witness were starting to arise. Between 2016 and 2019 a series of individuals were convicted of dishonestly engaging in selling carbon credits. A common factor in these cases was the use of a consistent expert witness, Andrew Ager.

In May 2019 Mr Ager was called upon again to give expert evidence in *Operation Balaban* heard at Southwark Crown Court. During the course of a *voir dire* Ager was discredited and abandoned as a witness by the prosecution on the grounds that it was accepted that he was not an expert of suitable calibre. During Mr Ager's cross examination in the *voir dire* it was established that he had received no training in the duties of being an expert, considered it was appropriate to withhold important concessions from the defence, held no relevant academic qualifications, made no attempt to comply with other obligations of an expert witness including failing to retain and reveal records and material, including material relevant to meetings he had attended[16].

In discharging the jury in the *Operation Balaban* trial the Judge drew from Lord Justice Goss' comments in Alex Pabon: *'This case stands as a stark reminder of the need for those instructing expert witnesses to satisfy themselves as to a witness' expertise and to engage (difficult though it*

16 [2021] EWCA Crim 107 at para 15

sometimes may be) an expert of a suitable calibre'. The Judge commented that time was to show that Andrew Ager was not an expert of a suitable calibre.

What followed was a series of appeals, conjoined due to a common theme, by Appellants who had all been convicted following trials in which Andrew Ager had given evidence. The Appellant's primary ground was that Mr Ager's failures highlighted in *Operation Balaban* undermined his evidence in their respective trials and therefore made their own convictions unsafe.

The Court of Appeal dismissed all appeals. They concluded that although Ager's lack of formal qualification should have been made clear it was not, by itself, determinative of whether he was entitled to give expert evidence. It was noted that Ager had some considerable experience in the financial commodity and carbon credits market. Further, as with the approach taken in *Pabon*, the court sought to consider how Mr Ager's failings in 2019 fit in with the evidence as a whole in relation to the convictions being appealed, coming back to the test of whether the convictions were consequently unsafe. It noted that there was no dispute to Ager's evidence in the other trials. There was no counter expert evidence (unlike in Balaban). The issue in the appellants' trials was participation. The Court reiterated that Ager's evidence was unchallenged. Ultimately the appeals were dismissed. It was considered untenable to conclude that the present convictions were unsafe because a witness in later proceedings could be demonstrated to have acted unprofessionally in the context of that case.

The independence of experts

Criminal Procedure Rule 19.2 outlines that the expert's duty lies to the court rather than the party who has instructed them.

Expert's duty to the court

19.2.—

> *(1) An expert must help the court to achieve the overriding objective—*
>
> *(a) by giving opinion which is— (i) objective and unbiased, and (ii) within the expert's area or areas of expertise; and*
>
> *(b) by actively assisting the court in fulfilling its duty of case management under rule 3.2, in particular by— (i) complying with directions made by the court, and (ii) at once informing the court of any significant failure (by the expert or another) to take any step required by such a direction.*
>
> *(2) This duty overrides any obligation to the person from whom the expert receives instructions or by whom the expert is paid.*

This overriding duty will often manifest itself in the expert's report in the form of a declaration confirming that the expert understands their duty is to help the court, by giving assistance by way of objective and unbiased opinion on matters within the expert's expertise, and that duty overrides any obligation towards the party by whom they are engaged or paid by.

It is well established that investigating officers can provide expert evidence[17]. In the conjoined appeals of *Myers, Cox and Brangman v R*[18] in which the Privy Council heard an appeal from the Court of Appeal for Bermuda Hughes SJC noted the following:

> *But the officer must have made a sufficient study, whether by formal training or through practical experience, to assemble what can properly be regarded as a balanced body of specialised knowledge which would not be available to the tribunal of fact. … But care must be taken that*

[17] See *R v Oakley* [1979] RTR 417 – "we would like to make it quite clear straight away that there is no question of a police officer being prevented from giving evidence as an expert if the subject in which he is giving evidence as an expert is a subject in which he has expert knowledge, and if it is restricted and directed to the issues in the case."

[18] [2016] AC 314

> *simple, and not necessarily balanced, anecdotal experience is not permitted to assume the robe of expertise. An example is given by the Canadian case Sekhon v The Queen [2014] 1 SCR 272 , where in the course of otherwise perfectly permissible expert evidence as to drug practices, there was adduced from the officer the fact that he had never encountered an innocent courier. That was clearly not a balanced, tested, or researched proposition as to the methods of drug importers, but simply his personal experience. It was not admissible and indeed proved nothing about the particular defendant on trial. Secondly, whilst a police officer may be an expert, by training or experience or both, if he is then he comes under the same duties to the court as does any other expert.*[19]

The court went on to note that compliance with the requirements of an expert may be difficult for a police officer who is combining the duties of an active investigator with providing independent expert evidence. Police witnesses who become expert witnesses should understand they are not part of the prosecution team but have separate independent duties to the court.

Police officers are entitled to give expert evidence on several different topics:

- Quality of driving – *Oakley*[20] – an officer with qualifications and experience in accident investigation can give evidence of how an accident occurred.

- Supply of drugs – *R v Hodges and Walker*[21] [2003] – an officer's evidence was capable of challenge during cross examination and by any evidence to the contrary adduced by the Defence.

[19] Ibid at para 58-59

[20] [1979] 70 Cr App R 7

[21] [2003] EWCA Crim 290

- Gang related evidence – see *R v Dixon-Kenton* [2021] EWCA Crim 673 where the Court of Appeal observed that expert evidence about the existence of gangs, their ways of operating, their language and culture is increasingly adduced in the courts. It was noted that police officers in several cities have developed expertise in the gang culture in the areas in which the officers operate. Referring to *Myers* it was noted that the admissibility of such evidence is well recognised.

Whilst a conflict of interest does not automatically disqualify the individual from giving expert evidence, where it is material and significant the court is unlikely to grant permission for the evidence to be called. Inevitably, any conflicts of interest must be disclosed so the matter can be addressed by either side.

CHAPTER TWO

THE USE OF EXPERT EVIDENCE IN CRIMINAL PROCEEDINGS

The admission of expert evidence at trial is a matter that ought to be properly case managed from the outset. Inevitably due to the complex nature of the material under consideration it can take many weeks if not months to provide a comprehensive expert report.

Case Management

Both the Magistrates' Court preparation for an effective trial form and the Crown Court PTPH form encourage the early identification of the need for expert evidence. Its introduction can have a significant effect on the progress of the case overall, including the duration of the trial and when the trial is set to take place.

Directions will often be tailored in respect the particular area of expertise on which evidence is sought – different areas of expertise have different timescales for completion of reports. Practitioners should have an idea of the likely timescales prior to setting directions to ensure they are realistic.

Often there will be competing experts on each side. Where this is the case directions may be set for a joint meeting with the production of a joint report identifying which issues are agreed between the experts and which are in dispute. This is aimed at assisting the court understand the key areas in dispute and enabling the advocates to focus attention on those areas. By contrast, civil proceedings encourage the production of a single joint expert report (a single expert, appointed by both, or all, parties to the proceedings) to assist the court on the issues.

Part 7 of the Criminal Practice Directions provides a draft timetable for the court's consideration in respect of obtaining medical reports for the purpose of sentencing, with a 6–8-week period between the hearing at which the expert is sought and the hearing at which the report is considered.

Criminal Procedure Rules

The formalities of what an expert report should contain can be found at Criminal Procedure Rule 19.4. This provides the following list of matters that must be addressed to make an expert report admissible:

> *(a) give details of the expert's qualifications, relevant experience and accreditation;*
>
> *(b) give details of any literature or other information which the expert has relied on in making the report;*
>
> *(c) contain a statement setting out the substance of all facts given to the expert which are material to the opinions expressed in the report, or upon which those opinions are based;*
>
> *(d) make clear which of the facts stated in the report are within the expert's own knowledge;*
>
> *(e) where the expert has based an opinion or inference on a representation of fact or opinion made by another person for the purposes of criminal proceedings (for example, as to the outcome of an examination, measurement, test or experiment)— (i) identify the person who made that representation to the expert, (ii) give the qualifications, relevant experience and any accreditation of that person, and (iii) certify that that person had personal knowledge of the matters stated in that representation;*
>
> *(f) where there is a range of opinion on the matters dealt with in the report— (i) summarise the range of opinion, and (ii) give reasons for the expert's own opinion;*

(g) *if the expert is not able to give an opinion without qualification, state the qualification;*

(h) *include such information as the court may need to decide whether the expert's opinion is sufficiently reliable to be admissible as evidence;*

(i) *contain a summary of the conclusions reached;*

(j) *contain a statement that the expert understands an expert's duty to the court, and has complied and will continue to comply with that duty; and*

(k) *contain the same declaration of truth as a witness statement.*[22]

It is worth noting the extensive list of requirements of the Criminal Procedure Rules for a full expert's report, with what is often contained in an SFR1 (Streamlined Forensic Report 1). Whilst an SFR1 will often be served with the initial details of a prosecution case to highlight the conclusions of a subsequent full expert report, it is not in itself an expert report. The purpose of an SFR1 is to provide the basis for admissions. In the absence of agreement, a full expert report in compliance with the requirements of the Criminal Procedure Rules ought to be provided as part of the prosecution case. It is therefore not possible to rely on the SFR1 as an expert's report (and therefore under the gateway of s30 Criminal Justice Act 1988 or s9 Criminal Justice Act 1967) in the absence of compliance with the criminal procedure rules.

Rule 19.6 provides that, where there is more than one expert giving evidence in relation to a matter in issue, those experts may discuss the issues in the proceedings and prepare a statement for the court setting out matters where they agree and disagree, and their respective reasons.

Furthermore, the court is provided with the discretion to direct a sole expert acting on behalf of all Defendants give expert evidence on an issue,

---

[22] Criminal Procedure Rules r19.4

rather than each Defendant calling their own separate expert to give evidence on the common issue.[23]

Where a challenge to the admissibility of the expert evidence is brought that ought to be done at the outset of the trial, potentially holding a *voir dire* on matters of evidence relevant to the issue of admissibility.[24] The burden rests on the party proffering the evidence to prove its admissibility.[25]

Expert Evidence and Unused Material

During the production of the expert's report, it is inevitable that material other than that in the final report will either be produced or referred to. This could be notes made during an experiment, or as part of the exercise in forming an opinion about what to include in the final report. The prosecution's obligations in relation to the collation and disclosure of unused material do not end with the material solely in the possession of the investigating agency but will encompass this material held by the third-party expert. In order to rely upon expert evidence obtained from experts who are not employed by the police, the prosecuting agency needs to ensure the third-party expert acts in compliance with the Criminal Procedure and Investigations Act 1996 (CPIA), so in turn the prosecuting agency can comply with their obligations. In order to do so the CPS will impose the obligations of the CPIA to retain, store and log the material that does not make its way into the final report through the contract entered into with the third-party expert.[26]

---

[23] Criminal Procedure rules r19.7

[24] R v Reed and others [2010] 1 Cr. App. R. 23

[25] R v Atkins and Atkins [2010] 1 Cr. App. R. 8 at 9

[26] See CPS Disclosure Manual chapter 36 available at: https://www.cps.gov.uk/sites/default/files/documents/legal_guidance/Disclosure-Manual-12-2018.pdf

The CPS have produced guidance for expert witnesses on their obligations in relation to unused material and case management[27]. The guidance notes that the obligations taken on by the expert in being instructed as an expert witness for the prosecution in criminal proceedings take precedence over any internal codes of practice or standards set by professional organisations.[28] Chapter 4 of the guidance provides the disclosure obligations of prosecution experts. It summarises the expert's obligations as *"retain, record and reveal."*[29]

The note highlights that the expert should retain everything produced during the case. Records of this material should be kept from the time of receipt of instructions and the duty to do so continues for the entirety of the time of the expert's involvement. That recorded material is required to be revealed to the prosecution team. The prosecution expert is required to confirm their understanding of the disclosure obligations to the court by signing a self-declaration as part of their statement. A suggested declaration is found in the Criminal Practice Direction at 19B.1.

The CPS require an expert to self-certify upon receipt of their instructions that they have read the 'CPS Guidance for Experts on Disclosure, Unused Material and Case Management'. It further confirms that the expert will disclosure matters required from them under the Criminal Procedure Rules. This certificate will be retained by the disclosure officer/investigating officer to show that the CPS have undertaken due diligence in the event matters go awry.

In relation to defence expert reports, rule 19.3 (c) notes that a party (whether prosecution or defence) serving the report should serve with it notice of anything known that might reasonably be thought capable of undermining the reliability of the expert's opinion or detracting from the credibility or impartiality of the expert. The other party (again whether

---

27 Available at https://www.cps.gov.uk/legal-guidance/cps-guidance-experts-disclosure-unused-material-and-case-management

28 Ibid at para 1.5

29 Ibid at 4.7

prosecution or defence) should have the opportunity to inspect any underlying records of examination and the like on which the findings in the report are based. A party that does not provide any material which underlies or might reasonably be thought capable of undermining the reliability of the opinion is at risk of the court directing that they may not introduce the expert evidence (r19.4).

Presentation of the Expert's Evidence

Whilst it will often be the case that the contents of the expert's report will be presented in the form of oral evidence directly from the expert to the trier of fact, it is also possible to provide the trier of fact with a copy of the report.

Section 30 of the Criminal Justice Act 1988 provides that an expert report is admissible as evidence in criminal proceedings, even if the expert does not attend to give oral evidence in those proceedings. However, to put the report before the trier of fact as evidence requires permission from the court. In determining whether to grant permission the court shall give consideration to the factors outlined in section 30(3) of the same act. Those factors are:

- the contents of the report,
- the reason why it is proposed that the person making the report shall not give oral evidence (if applicable),
- any risk, having regard to the contents of the report, of unfairness to the accused, and
- to any other circumstances that appear to the court to be relevant.

The section provides for two things: firstly for the written report to be provided to supplement the expert's oral evidence (in a manner akin to a tier of fact being provided with an ordinary witnesses witness statement whilst listening to their oral evidence on the same matter), or secondly for the expert report to be adduced absent the oral evidence of the expert (a hearsay application). In the same way that the hurdle for adducing hearsay evidence going to the sole or decisive issue in a case is a high one, it is unlikely that a judge will readily utilise their discretion to allow unchallenged expert evidence going directly to a relevant matter in issue to go before the trier of fact. There is perhaps greater room for argument in cases involving experts on both sides, where the opposing expert can challenge the contents of the absent expert's report. If the report is allowed to be put before the trier of fact the advocate then faces the presentational challenge of ensuring it is understood. The inherent benefit of having an expert in the witness box being clearly and concisely questioned and challenged will be missing in such an instance.

However, presentationally this provides challenges for the party seeking to adduce evidence of the absent expert's report. Whilst the trier of fact reading the material may well be one thing, ensuring understanding and clarity that is obtained through a clear and concise examination in chief is quite different.

Section 127 of the Criminal Justice Act 2003 provides that an expert can give evidence of opinion based on the preparatory work of others where those others have prepared statements in respect of their work. In many experts' reports assistants will have been used to conduct work that feeds into the final report. The Defence can oppose this approach and seek an order from the court that it is not in the interests of justice for the expert to give evidence of others work. In deciding whether to grant such an order the court will consider the matters outlined at s127(5), namely the expense of calling those assistants, what relevant evidence they can give and whether the assistants can reasonably be expected to remember the matters stated well enough to give oral evidence of them. Where there is root and branch challenge to the expert's conclusions, the defence should not be afraid to seek an order under this section requiring the attendance at court of those individuals whose work has fed into the final conclusions.

Use of Illustrations and Animation

Almost inevitably the expert's report will contain complex matters of fact and opinion. The presentation of such evidence, in a manner that is accessible to the lay trier of fact is part of the skill of the advocate. However, the presentation of the expert's report is not limited to the spoken word. It has been considered perfectly proper for the expert to use graphics to assist in presenting their opinion.

In R v Metcalfe[30] the prosecution's expert used a series of animations to illustrate their opinion on how a death had occurred. The decision to utilise animation as part of the presentation of the expert's evidence was challenged by the Defence as unfair within the terms of section 78 of the Police and Criminal Evidence Act 1984. Having allowed the animations to be used in the trial, the decision not to exclude was challenged in the Court of Appeal. The higher court held that the animations were an illustration of the expert's opinion and not any form of independent scientific evidence (as was argued) and therefore the credibility of the animations ran in parallel to the credibility of the expert's opinion, rather than as a separate source of independent scientific evidence.

Where the conclusions drawn in the report can be better understood through the use of graphics (for example, in re-enactment cases) the expert should not avoid the use of that form of presentational device in order to assist understanding. The boundary rests where the graphic goes beyond the conclusion of the point made by the expert, which will often be found in explanatory comments and labels on the diagram, which whilst inadvertent may well be inadmissible.

30 [2016] EWCA Crim 681

Determining the Reliability of Expert Opinion

Whilst the reliability and conclusions of each expert will depend on the individual report, the Criminal Practice Directions highlight a number of factors which can be taken into account for consideration of the reliability of the expert's opinion[31]. These are:

- *The extent and quality of the data on which the expert's opinion is based, and the validity of the methods by which they were obtained,*
- *Whether the opinion formed by the expert is based on inference, and if so how reliable that inference is,*
- *If the opinion relies on the results of experimentation, whether the opinion takes into account any degrees of precision or margins of uncertainty affecting the accuracy of the experiment,*
- *The extent to which any material relied upon by the expert in forming their opinion has been reviewed by others with relevant expertise and whether it stands up to scrutiny,*
- *The extent to which the expert's opinion is based on material falling outside their own field of expertise,*
- *Whether any relevant information was not considered by the expert,*
- *Whether there is a range of expert opinion on a topic,*
- *Whether the expert's methods follow established practice*

The practice direction goes on to provide that a party seeking to adduce expert evidence is required to give notice of anything that they are aware

[31] Criminal Practice Direction part 5 at 19A.5

of which might reasonably be thought capable of undermining the reliability of the expert's opinion or credibility[32]. This includes any adverse judicial comment towards the expert's evidence[33], and any case in which an appeal has been allowed by reason of faults in the expert's evidence.

Directing the Jury on Expert Evidence

The directions given to the trier of fact in relation to the evidence of an expert need to be carefully crafted to the particular evidence given by the expert and its application to the case.

The Crown Court compendium provides judges with some support.[34] It highlights that once the expert witness and the issues to which their evidence goes have been identified, the Judge should make clear that expert witnesses are regularly required to give evidence to assist juries on matters outside their knowledge. It explains that the jury's task is to weigh up the evidence, decide what they accept and what they do not, taking into account the qualifications of the expert and the methods by which their opinion is formed. Importantly it highlights that the expert evidence is only part of the evidence of the case, and that the jury must consider all the evidence before reaching their verdict.

There is an important need to not only summarise what the expert says, but also how the jury should treat the expert evidence. In the conjoined appeals *Henderson v The Crown*[35] the Court of Appeal considered three cases of shaken baby syndrome. In assessing how the trial Judge summed up the expert evidence to the jury in one of the appeals the Court had the following to say:

---

[32] Ibid at 19A.7

[33] See for example DPP v Walsall Magistrates' Court [2019] EWHC 3317 (Admin) at para 69

[34] Crown Court Bench Book, as amended June 2022 – see chapter 10-3

[35] [2010] EWCA Crim 1269

> *114. The summing-up was also defective in its structure. The Judge carefully and conscientiously recited long passages of the expert evidence to the jury. But he did not 'direct' the jury at all. He recited those passages in the chronological order in which the evidence was given. That was of little assistance to the jury.*
>
> *115. The jury required a careful direction as to the essential issues which they had to determine and a reminder of that evidence and only that evidence which went to those issues. It was necessary to deal with that evidence issue by issue.*[36]

Expert evidence will be called by a party for a reason. That reason will be that it goes to the heart of an issue in the trial that is disputed between the parties. The Court of Appeal has provided clear guidance to Judges that when summing up an expert's evidence it is not good enough to simply recite the evidence given by the expert, but to highlight how that evidence goes to the issues in contention between the parties.

In the same case it was noted:

> *In cases where it is relevant to do so, they should be reminded that medical science develops and that which was previously thought unknown may subsequently be recognised and acknowledged. As it was put by Toulson LJ, "today's orthodoxy may become tomorrow's outdated learning" (R v Holdsworth [2008] EWCA Crim 971 at [57]). In cases where developing medical science is relevant, the jury should be reminded that special caution is needed where expert opinion evidence is fundamental to the prosecution [57].*[37]

Science develops. What may have been an approved procedure in 2020 may not be the same in 2030. Advocates may seek to take advantage of that. But that approach requires the need for caution. Where there may be developments in the science, that does not extend to guesswork as to what the future holds. The forensic sciences are developing fields, and

---

[36] Ibid at para 114 – 115

[37] Ibid at para 217

with advances in technology, methodology and knowledge, what may have been orthodoxy today may not be tomorrow. But when summing up a case the extent for caution does not extend to warning the jury about theoretical future changes in the field of expertise, particularly where the modern science or medicine is stable.[38]

[38] See Syeda Begum v Her Majesty's Advocate [2020] HCJAC 16, referencing *Henderson* at para 52

CHAPTER THREE

AN INTRODUCTION TO THE USE OF PSYCHIATRIC EVIDENCE IN THE CRIMINAL JUSTICE SYSTEM

> *"Throughout history, seriously anti-social acts, particularly acts of violence, have been committed by people whose mental capacity was such that they were not responsible, or not fully responsible, for their acts, or could not fairly be required to stand trial. Such cases pose an inescapable public, moral and human rights dilemma: for while such people may present a continuing danger from which the public deserve to be protected, it would be offensive to visit the full rigour of the law on those who are not mentally responsible, or not able to defend themselves, as an ordinary person of sound mind would be taken to be, and who may (despite their mental incapacity) have done nothing wrong or dangerous."*[39]

Over 20 years since the House of Lords made the above comment in *R v Antoine* the courts are still trying to find the correct balance between the public, moral and human rights dilemmas in treating and sentencing people who suffer from mental health conditions.

Awareness of an individual's mental health has increased in recent years as society becomes more aware of the needs of those suffering from mental health concerns. As society's understanding of these issues grows, so does the need for adaption and acknowledgement by the criminal courts of how these issues can lead to criminal behaviour but more

[39] R v Antoine [2001] AC 340 at 344

importantly how treatment and rehabilitation can be provided to mitigate against the risk of repetition.

Cases where mental health factors arise can broadly be separated into two issues: those where an individual's mental health condition affected their ability to carry out the criminal offence in question, and those where the individual's mental health condition affects their ability to participate in the trial. These two situations are broadly encompassed through provisions relating to the common law defence of 'insanity' and the procedural provisions for determining 'fitness to plead'.

Either instance requires the involvement of psychiatric evidence. A psychiatrist is a medically qualified individual who specialises in the prevention, diagnosis, and treatment of mental illness. A psychologist by comparison specialises in the examination of human behaviour upon assessment of the emotional, cognitive, and mental processes of an individual.

Shortly after publication of the first edition of this book the Sentencing Council published guidelines, in the form of overarching principles, to assist Judges sentence cases involving offenders with mental disorders, developmental disorders or neurological impairments.

Unlike offence specific guidelines, the guidelines relating to mental disorders do not provide sentencing judges with a range of answers to the question of sentencing, but instead provides an educational piece, setting out factors that ought to be considered prior to the sentencing exercise as well as highlighting the range of powers that a sentencer has when dealing with someone who suffers from a mental disorder. It attempts to deal with mental health myths, for example that no adverse inference should necessarily be drawn if an offender had not previously either been formally diagnosed or willing to disclose an impairment or disorder.

The new guidelines put the sentencer in the best possible position to understand the interaction between the mental disorder and the offending, and how the usual sentencing factors should be adapted to accommodate the impact of the mental disorder on the sentence to be passed.

CHAPTER FOUR

FITNESS TO PLEAD

The fitness to plead procedure is an area that most practitioners will have come across during their practice. In general terms the fitness to plead process assesses a defendant's state of mind at the time of the assessment (rather than at the time of the act or omission alleged to have taken place) to consider whether they are able to follow and participate in the proceedings brought against them.

Whilst an individual's state of mental health may be in flux, it is important that practitioners are able to identify at the earliest possible stage where the possibility of unfitness to plead arises due to the procedural hurdles required to be passed as part of the process. This is particularly so as an individual can move between being fit and unfit to plead during the life of the proceedings.

The case of *R. v Pritchard*[40] provides the foundation for the test for fitness to plead. The parts of that judgment that remain of relevance to the test for fitness to plead are that, where a court has been asked to determine a defendant's fitness to plead, it must consider the following criteria:

> *whether [the defendant] can plead to the indictment or not; ... whether he is of sufficient intellect to comprehend the course of proceedings on the trial, so as to make a proper defence – to know that he might challenge any of you to whom he may object – and to comprehend the details of the evidence*[41].

---

40 [1836] 173 ER 135

41 Ibid at 135

The Pritchard criteria continue to be applied today, although in a slightly fleshed out form. *R v M (John)*[42] outlined six key capacities in order to be fit to plead:

- The ability to understand the charges;
- The ability to decide whether to plead guilty;
- The ability to exercise the right to challenge a juror;
- The capacity to instruct solicitors and counsel;
- The capacity to follow the course of proceedings; and
- The capacity to give evidence in his or her defence.[43]

Where a Defendant lacks one or more of these factors, it provides an indication that the Defendant is unfit to plead.

Unfitness to plead is not always a permanent finding and can lead the trial against the defendant being postponed until such a time as the defendant is fit to plead. The way the issue of fitness to plead is raised depends on in which court is pursued.

<u>Expert Evidence on Unfitness to Plead</u>

It is crucial that a psychiatrist has in mind the test for fitness to plead when interviewing the defendant and preparing the expert report.[44] This is so since even in situations where the defendant is found to have a very

---

[42] [2003] EWCA Crim 3452

[43] Ibid at paragraph 20

[44] *R. v Walls (Robert)*, [2011] 2 Cr. App. R. 6, para. 29: "[Dr Clark] had failed to address the Pritchard criteria in his report… [w]e very much regret to have to conclude that we found Dr Clark a somewhat unsatisfactory witness on whose evidence we could not, on analysis, place reliance.

severe mental illness they may nevertheless be properly capable of participating in their own trial.[45] Even where a defendant is found to be incapable of acting in their best interests, it may be that they are nevertheless fit to plead.[46] An expert psychiatrist should therefore be directed to the expanded Pritchard criteria set in *R v M (John)*.

A defendant's fitness to plead should be distinguished from their ability to give evidence. As outlined in *R v Patrick Orr*[47] the provisions of section 35(1)(a) of the Criminal Justice and Public Order Act 1994 address situations where a defendant's physical or mental condition make it undesirable for him to give evidence (and be cross examined). This is in contrast to the defendant being able to understand the questions they are asked, apply their mind to answering them and convey the answers in an intelligible manner (which are matters going to fitness to plead).

The psychiatric report should be as contemporaneous with the trial as is possible.[48] One corollary of this is that it is "very rare indeed" for an *ex post facto* determination from an expert to persuade the court that the defendant, having faced trial, had not in fact been fit to plead.[49] This is particularly so since there is a distinct responsibility for the trial judge to raise the issue of fitness to plead if it is considered appropriate.[50] It is therefore difficult to raise the issue of fitness on appeal,[51] although an appeal on the grounds of fitness was successful in *R. v Chitolie*[52], where a conviction was substituted with a finding that the applicant did the acts

---

45 See *R v Berry (John)* (1978) 66 Cr.App. R. 156.

46 See R v *Robertson* (1968) 52 Cr. App. R., p.694.

47 [2016] EWCA Crim 889

48 *R. v Erskine; R. v Williams* [2009] EWCA Crim 1425.

49 *Ibid.*

50 *Ibid.*

51 Although see *R. v Grant (Liam William)* [2008] EWCA Crim 1870, where the appeal was allowed, and a supervision order was substituted for a community order.

52 [2016] EWCA Crim 14

he was charged with.[53] In that case, the conviction was quashed and substituted with an hospital order with a restriction order.

Qualification/Approval of Medical Experts

The requirement under Criminal Procedure (Insanity) Act 1964 that one of the two medical experts be "duly approved" is a requirement that they are approved under section 12(2) of the Mental Health Act 1983. This requires that they are "a practitioner approved for the purposes of this section by the Secretary of State as having special experience in the diagnosis or treatment of mental disorder." A practitioner who has received such approval is referred to as an approved clinician.

Section 12ZA of the Mental Health Act 1983 provides the Secretary of State can enter into agreement with another for the purposes of authorising individuals under section 12. Each region in England and Wales has an approval panel which determines whether a medical practitioner can be an approved clinician. For example, the responsibility for approving doctors in London is exercised be Central and North West London NHS Foundation Trust on behalf of the Secretary of State. To obtain approval on the panels the Secretary of State has issued guidance under the catchily named 'Mental Health Act 1983 Instructions with Respect to the Exercise of an Approval Function in relation to section 12 Doctors 2015.'[54] The instructions provide the qualification requirements to become section 12 registered, which include having a minimum of four years full time experience in a relevant post, provide references from those already s12 approved, and completed an induction training course.[55] The period of approval is for five years, subject to renewal.

---

53 *R. v Marcantonio* [2016] EWCA Crim 14, para. 104.

54 Available at: https://assets.publishing.service.gov.uk/government/uploads/system/uploads/attachment_data/file/489217/2015_s12_Instructions.pdf

55 Mental Health Act 1983 Instructions with Respect to the Exercise of an Approval Function in relation to Section 12 Doctors 2015 part 1 section 3

Remand to Hospital to Report on the Accused's mental condition

In addition to section 11 of the Powers of Criminal Courts (Sentencing) Act 2000 (in respect of the Magistrates' Court and addressed above) section 35 of the Mental Health Act 1983 allows either the Crown Court or a magistrates' court to remand a defendant to hospital for the purposes of completing a report on the mental health of the defendant. In relation to Crown Court proceedings this section allows remand for any person who has been arraigned but not yet sentenced. In the magistrates' court this section can be used for any person convicted of an offence punishable by imprisonment, and any person who the court is satisfied did the act or made the omission charged. The court when exercising this power however must receive written or oral evidence of a registered medical practitioner, giving reason to suspect the accused person is suffering from a mental disorder, and that a place is available for the accused's admission to hospital. Additionally, the court must be of the view it would be impracticable for a mental health report to be made if the Defendant were on bail.

Remand shall take place for no more than 28 days at a time, but this can be extended if it is considered necessary for completing the assessment. However, the total period of time an accused can be remanded under this section is no more than 12 weeks in all.

Should an accused abscond from the hospital where they are being remanded, they can be arrested and brought to court at which point the court may terminate the remand under this section and deal with the accused in any way in which they could have dealt with them had they not been remanded under s35.

Fitness to Plead Proceedings in the Crown Court

For proceedings in the Crown Court, the fitness to plead process can be found in the Criminal Procedure (Insanity) Act 1964.

Timing: The issue of fitness to plead should be determined as soon as the required information is before the court. However its determination may be postponed until any time before the opening of the defence case (if raised at a point prior to this).[56] A finding of unfitness can be made up to the point where a jury return a verdict of acquittal on the count(s) being tried.[57] If the issue is raised during the trial, the judge may well adjourn proceedings to allow for a psychiatric report to be obtained by the defence to pursue this course rather than proceed with the trial.[58]

Where potential unfitness to plead is identified prior to the Plea and Trial Preparation ('PTPH') stage, arraignment will often be adjourned at the PTPH with the usual stage dates set, with additional directions built in for the service of experts' reports and a further case management hearing ('FCMH'). The court will often be reluctant to make progress with the case overall whilst the issue of fitness to plead is considered. This is particularly so given that if the Defendant is found unfit to plead a 'trial of the facts' will need to take place in front of a jury.

Who determines the issue? Since the passing into force of the Domestic Violence, Crime and Victims Act 2004, the issue of fitness to plead is to be determined by the judge and not the jury.[59]

How is the issue determined? Determination of the issue requires the written or oral evidence of two or more registered medical practitioners, at least one of whom is duly approved.[60] An approved practitioner is one approved by the Secretary of State as a practitioner who has experience in the diagnosis and treatment of mental disorders under section 12(2) of the Mental Health Act 1983.

Where the parties' experts are in dispute over whether the defendant is fit to plead or not, in anticipation of a contested hearing to determine the issue, the court will often direct that a discussion take place between the experts to narrow the issues in dispute. One thing that might be

---

56 Criminal Procedure (Insanity) Act 1964, at section 4(2).

57 Ibid at section 4(3)

58 See e.g. *R. v Orr (Patrick Neale)*, [2016] 2 Cr. App. R. 32, para. 14.

59 Criminal Procedure (Insanity) Act 1964, section 4(5).

60 Criminal Procedure (Insanity) Act 1964, section 4(6).

considered is whether, from their position as experts, they are aware of medical practitioners who might be better placed to determine the issues of dispute. If the issue is the extent of a cognitive impairment, for example, the appropriate way forward might be to instruct a neuropsychologist. Where there is a dispute as to physical damage caused to the brain it might be that instructing a neurologist to determine the issue is appropriate.

Where following discussions there remains an irresolvable conflict between the positions of the defence and prosecution experts, the issue of fitness to plead will be determined by way of a contested oral hearing. It is not envisaged that the defendant will have to give evidence at that hearing, since the subject of the hearing will be whether the defendant is in fact capable of participating in their own trial, but there is no prohibition against this.

Whether the Defence have instructed two practitioners who both agree that the defendant is unfit to plead, or the evidence of unfitness comes from both prosecution and defence instructed experts, it is not the case that the judge has to accept the recommendations of the psychiatrists. This is the case even if no evidence is presented recommending the defendant is fit to plead. The psychiatric expert evidence is just one part of the evidence that must be considered.[61] This is so since considerations other than the mental disability of a defendant are relevant, such as their age, or their possession of a particularly low IQ.[62] Indeed, a defendant with no history of psychological illness could be unfit to plead.[63] As noted in *R v Robert Walls: "A court would be failing in its duty both to the public and defendant if it did not rigorously examine the evidence and reach its own conclusion."*[64]

---

[61] See *R. v Walls (Robert)* [2011] 2 Cr. App. R. 6, paras 35 – 36.

[62] Ibid at para. 24.

[63] n.47

[64] n.47 at para 38

Following hearing live evidence of medical professionals, the judge will proceed to decide on whether the defendant is in fact under a disability such that he is unfit to plead.

Burden and Standard of Proof: Where the issue of fitness to plead is raised by the prosecution, it is for them to prove the defendant is unfit to the criminal standard. Where the issue is raised by the defence it is for them to prove it to the civil standard. However, where the issue is raised independently by the court, the prosecution must prove that the defendant is fit to plead to the criminal standard.

Procedure following a finding of unfitness: The procedure to be followed after a finding of unfitness to plead is found in section 4A of the Criminal Procedure (Insanity) Act 1964. Where a defendant is found to be unfit to plead, they shall not face a trial, but a jury will determine whether the defendant committed the act or omission he is charged with.[65] This is based on any evidence presented by the prosecution and defence. This process is known as a trial of the facts. If the defendant is found unfit during a trial, that jury will be the same jury that was trying them in the ordinary way.[66] The jury will not need to determine any issue of *mens rea*, but must make a determination as to whether the defendant committed the *actus reus* of the offence.[67] If they are satisfied the defendant committed the act they will return a finding that the accused did the act or made the omission charged against him. If they are not satisfied, they shall return a verdict of acquittal as if the count in question had proceeded to conclusion in a conventional trial.

[65] Criminal Procedure (Insanity) Act 1964, section 4A(2).

[66] Criminal Procedure (Insanity) Act 1964, section 4A(5).

[67] Criminal Procedure (Insanity) Act 1964, section 4A(2).

The Act's Hearing

Having established that a defendant is unfit to plead (and thereby provide instructions to their Counsel) the case proceeds with the prosecution calling evidence in order to establish that the actus reus of an offence has taken place.

The hearing under section 4A Criminal Procedure (Insanity) Act 1964 is a criminal proceeding, and therefore the same rules of evidence apply[68]. As was noted by Lord Bingham in *R v H*[69] "*the procedure under section 4A must always, of course, be conducted with scrupulous regard for the interests of the accused person*". Given the accused person's ability to defend themselves against the accusation is curtailed by virtue of their mental state through no fault of their own evidential applications and the like ought to be given rigorous scrutiny.

If there is objective evidence raising the issue of mistake, accident, or self-defence then it is open for the jury to conclude that the defendant did not do the act. However, in the absence of objective evidence the defence cannot raise such an issue and invite the jury to acquit[70] Objective evidence may include eyewitnesses, CCTV, or injuries received by the defendant (for example, in an allegation of assault).

What is said in interview may be relied upon if it can be established that, though unfit to stand trial, observations made at interview were not affected by the subsequent impairment to their mental state[71]. The court will usually need to be persuaded through expert evidence that the defendant understood the caution and it was appropriate to interview them. If an interview is admitted, whether in full or in part, it is likely that the Judge will need to give a carefully crafted direction warning the jury of the need for particular care and that what was said in interview

---

68 R v Chal [2007] EWCA Crim 2647

69 [2003] 2 Cr App R 2

70 Antoine [2001] 1 AC 340

71 R v Swinbourne [2013] EWCA Crim 2329

may be as a result of the defendant's disability rather than because they were lying or attempting to mislead the police.

Transitioning between unfitness and fitness between the s4A hearing and disposal

Having found that an individual did the act it is likely that the court will adjourn disposal of the case in order to seek the recommendation of medical professionals as to the appropriate disposal of the case under s5 of the Criminal Procedure (Insanity) Act 1964.

As set out above a state of unfitness is not fixed. An individual can fluctuate between unfitness and fitness to plead during the life of the proceedings. So, what approach should the court take if an individual becomes fit to plead following the s4A hearing but before the s5 disposal?

The position was considered by the Divisional Court in R (Hasani) v Crown Court at Blackfriars[72]. Hasani was determined to be unfit to plead following a hearing under s4 Criminal Procedure (Insanity) Act 1964 in relation to proceedings alleging wounding and assault. Having been found to have committed the acts amounting to wounding and assault the case was adjourned for further reports on disposal. During the course of this examination the defendant became fit to plead. The Crown Court considered that the appropriate route at that stage was to have the defendant arraigned and proceed to a trial. By way of Judicial Review, the decision that it would be inappropriate in those circumstances to pass an absolute discharge under s5(2) (disposals following a finding of unfitness to plead), was challenged.

The High Court concluded that the sections 4A and 5 procedures are inapplicable if, following a further section 4 hearing (determination of fitness to plead) the court concludes that the accused person is fit to plead.[73] The court considered that if, upon a subsequent finding of fitness under s4 the case will proceed to arraignment and the normal trial

72 [2005] EWHC 3016 (Admin).

73 Ibid, see para 14

process will follow. Consequently the court was not limited to the disposals under s5(2).

Appealing a finding under s4 to the Court of Appeal from the Crown Court

Section 15 of the Criminal Appeals Act 1968 provides that a person may appeal to the Court of Appeal a finding that they are unfit to plead and/or they did the act or omission charged against them. In order to appeal leave is required from the Court of Appeal, or, within 28 days of the finding of unfitness a certificate from the trial Judge confirming that the matter is suitable for appeal.

Criminal Procedure Rule 39.4 deals with the procedure for applying for a certificate from the Crown Court Judge. It notes that an application can be made orally immediately following the decision that is subject to appeal, or in writing no more than 14 days following the decision.

There is, in contrast, no right of appeal against a finding that an individual is fit to plead. The decision to find fitness to plead neither falls within the ambit of section 15 of the act nor section 1 of the same act providing the general provision for appealing a conviction.

An accused found to be unfit to plead is not considered competent to bring an appeal against the finding of unfitness. When a finding of unfitness is made, the advocate acting on behalf of the Defendant becomes court appointed to protect the individual's interests at the subsequent acts hearing. At the conclusion of the proceedings the individual is duty bound to consider whether there are any grounds to appeal the decision to find unfitness. If not, there is no valid ground to consider appeal as the person subject to the ruling is not considered competent to properly bring an appeal. However, if the person does launch an appeal the Criminal Appeals Office will ensure it receives judicial consideration.

Where a finding of unfitness is considered unsafe the appeal will be allowed, otherwise it will be dismissed[74]. Where an appeal is allowed on the basis the defendant could not be said to be unfit, the case will be tried in the normal way. Where an appeal is successful against the finding that the Defendant did the act or omission charged the Court of Appeal will record an acquittal.[75]

'Fitness to Plead' in the Magistrates' and Youth Court

The procedure as set out in the Criminal Procedure (Insanity) Act 1964 is not applicable in the magistrates' court. Insofar as there is a formal procedure, it may be found in section 37(3) of the Mental Health Act 1983 and section 11 of the Powers of Criminal Courts (Sentencing) Act 2000.

Section 37(3) of the Mental Health Act 1983 provides the following:

> *(3) Where a person is charged before a magistrates' court with any act or omission as an offence and the court would have power, on convicting him of that offence, to make an order under subsection (1) above in his case, then, if the court is satisfied that the accused did the act or made the omission charged, the court may, if it thinks fit, make such an order without convicting him.*

Section 11 (1) of the Powers of Criminal Courts (Sentencing) Act 2000 provides that:

> *(1) If, on the trial by a magistrates' court of an offence punishable on summary conviction with imprisonment, the court—*
>
> > *(a) is satisfied that the accused did the act or made the omission charged, but*

74 Section 16(3) Criminal Appeal Act 1968

75 Section 16(4) Criminal Appeal Act 1968

> (b) *is of the opinion that an inquiry ought to be made into his physical or mental condition before the method of dealing with him is determined,*
>
> *the court shall adjourn the case to enable a medical examination and report to be made, and shall remand him.*

The procedure only applies where the magistrates court is trying an offence punishable on summary conviction with imprisonment.[76] Whilst the legislation outlines that the magistrates' court, where upon finding that the accused did the act or made the omission charged, shall then adjourn the case to enable reports to be prepared, where the issue of fitness to plead has been identified at an earlier stage it will be expected that steps have already been taken to obtain reports. That will result in the 'trial' in effect being a 'trial of fact' as per the Crown Court procedure.

Where the court does adjourn the case for consideration of the Defendant's fitness that should not be for longer than four weeks if remanded on bail, or three weeks if remanded into custody[77]

If the accused is then remanded on bail, a condition must be imposed that he undergoes a medical examination or, where the court so directs, examination by two medical practitioners.[78] The correct approach is that two medical practitioners must be consulted since, in order for the court to make a hospital order or other appropriate disposal, the evidence of two registered medical practitioners is required.[79] Where it is anticipated that a hospital order may be appropriate, one medical practitioner should be an approved clinician under section 12(2) of the Mental Health Act 1983.

---

[76] Powers of Criminal Courts (Sentencing) Act 2000, section 11(1).

[77] Powers of Criminal Courts (Sentencing) Act 2000, section 11(2)

[78] Powers of Criminal Courts (Sentencing) Act 2000, section 11(3)(a).

[79] Mental Health Act 1983, section 37(2).

Upon receipt of evidence from two medical practitioners, if the court is satisfied that the defendant is suffering from a mental disorder of a nature and degree that makes detention in a hospital appropriate it may impose a hospital order. If a restriction order ought to be attached to the hospital order the magistrates' court can commit the matter to the Crown Court for sentence.

Because there is no formal conviction in the Magistrates' Court it is not possible to appeal against 'conviction'. However, where a hospital order is made, an appeal against that order lies with the Crown Court.

CHAPTER FIVE

INSANITY

Whereas fitness to plead focuses on whether an individual can follow the criminal proceedings, insanity looks at the Defendant's mental state at the time of the incident that is alleged to amount to criminal conduct. It therefore acts as a defence to the proceedings.

The criminal justice system has recognised insanity for over 200 years. An early example of the recognition of insanity is found in *Arnold's Case*[80] in which the defendant attempted (unsuccessfully) to rely on insanity having shot Lord Onslow. Debates surrounding insanity continued through *Hadfield's Case*[81] in which the defendant had tried to assassinate King George III, subsequently being acquitted on the grounds of insanity.

Whilst the present provision for returning a verdict of insanity by the jury is found in the Trial of Lunatics Act 1883[82], over 80 years before the passing of that act the Criminal Lunatics Act 1800[83] provided:

> *"That in all cases where it shall be given in evidence upon the trial of any person charged with treason, murder, or felony, that such person was insane at the time of the commission of such offence, and such person shall be acquitted, the jury shall be required to find specially whether such person was insane at the time of the commission of such offence, and to declare whether such person was acquitted by them on account of such insanity; and if they shall find that such person was insane at the time of the committing such offence, the court before*

---

80 {1724) 16 State Tr 695

81 (1800) 27 State Tr 1281

82 As amended by the Criminal Procedure (Insanity) Act 1964

83 Criminal Lunatics Act 1800 (39 & 40 Geo 3, c 94)

> *whom such trial shall be had, shall order such person to be kept in strict custody, in such place and in such manner as to the court shall seem fit, until his Majesty's pleasure shall be known ..."*

However, between the Trial of Lunatics Act 1883 and the Criminal Lunatics Act 1800 came the well-known case of M'Naghten[84]. What amounts to insanity is still found in the judgment of M'Naghten:

> *"jurors ought to be told that every man is to be presumed to be sane, and to possess a sufficient degree of reason to be responsible for his crimes, until the contrary be proved to their satisfaction: and that to establish a defence on the ground of insanity, it must be clearly proved that at the time of the committing the act the party accused was labouring under such a defect of reason, from disease of the mind, as not to know the nature and quality of the act he was doing, or, as not to know that what he was doing was wrong."*[85]

There are two limbs to the insanity defence, either of which will allow the defence to be raised:

- If, by reason of disease of the mind, the Defendant did not know the nature and quality of the act (a denial of the *mens rea)*, or

- If even the defendant did know the nature and quality of the act, because of the disease of the mind they did not know it was wrong.

The first limb refers to the physical nature and quality of the act, and not its moral or legal quality (for example, where A kills B under an insane delusion they are breaking a jar).

The second limb means legally wrong, and not morally wrong (albeit, not to be confused with ignorance of the law, and subject to clarification

---

84 M'Naghten's Case (1843) 10 Clark and Finnelly 200, 210, (1843) 8 ER 718, [1843-60] All ER Rep 229.

85 Ibid.

in R v Keal for which see below). If a person does something they know is legally wrong, but believes it morally justified they will not succeed on a plea of insanity. However, if a person kills someone believing they are killing a mythological figure the defence may well be open to them. An example of the second limb given in *Loake v CPS*[86]

> *"if a man repeatedly telephones his neighbour at all hours of the day and night in an attempt to perform a religious conversion, in the deluded belief that he has received a divine order to do so, and that it is lawful to comply, then he is not guilty by reason of insanity under the second limb of the M'Naghten Rules. That would be so, notwithstanding that he has committed the* actus reus *of the offence and his conduct, viewed objectively, amounts to harassment. Such a man does not know that what he is doing is wrong and therefore as a matter of principle should not be subject to criminal punishment."*[87]

A malfunctioning of the mind may be caused by internal and external factors. Insanity considers internal factors. External factors that cause a malfunctioning of the mind may lead to a complete acquittal on the ground of non-insane automatism, considered later in this chapter. The psychiatrist will be able to assist in assessing the defendant will be to consider the cause of the malfunctioning of the mind to ensure the correct approach is taken by the practitioner, and further expert evidence obtained if appropriate.

In relation to the second limb, the question of what was meant by 'wrong' in M'Naughten was considered in *R v Jonathan Keal*[88]. The Appellant, Mr Keal, had been convicted of three counts of attempted murder and sentenced to a hospital order under s37 with restriction under s41. An appeal was heard on the basis of the Judge's directions in relation to the issue of insanity, and how the issue of whether a defendant knows what they were doing was correctly directed. The Court in *Keal* set out that in

---

86 [2017] EWHC 2855 (Admin)

87 Ibid at para 55

88 [2022] EWCA Crim 341

order to establish the defence of insanity within the M'Naghten rules on the grounds of not knowing the act was wrong they must establish both that (a) they did not know that the act was unlawful (contrary to the law) and (b) that the act was morally wrong (wrong by the standards of ordinary people). Wrong was interpreted to mean both against the law and by standards of ordinary people.

The court went on to consider the issue of choice and whether the M'Naghten rules include an element of a 'lack of choice'. It rejected the submission that that concept of knowledge of wrongdoing imported an element of choice. Relying on, amongst other things, the Law Commissions 2013 report into the defence of insanity, the Court noted that the recommendations for a defence of 'irresistible impulse' had not been adopted.

Burden and Standard of Proof

When insanity is raised by the Defence it is for the defendant to prove on the balance of probabilities that he or she was insane at the time of the incident within the M'Naghten test. The prosecution may call evidence to disprove the assertion and will only succeed if there is no reasonable belief that the accused was not insane at the time of the incident.[89]

In exceptional circumstances, considering the course of the proceedings, the Judge may raise the issue of insanity of their own volition[90]. Where this is done, both sides should be given an opportunity to call relevant evidence on the issue, even if that necessitates an adjournment so that such evidence can be obtained. Although there is no requirement in law to put expert evidence before the jury in order that it may reach the 'special verdict', it would be unusual if the court did not require the expert evidence of a mental health professional to address the issue of insanity. The mental health of a defendant is precisely the sort of thing

---

89 R v Dickie [1984] 1 WLR 1031

90 Ibid

that falls outside the 'common knowledge and experience' of the jury and so it would be anticipated that expert evidence should be adduced.

Insanity in the Crown Court

The Trial of Lunatics Act 1883 provides that a jury may find a Defendant not guilty by reason of insanity where they find the Defendant was insane at the time of undertaking the act or omission amounting to the charge.

Section 2 of the act provides:

> *Where in any indictment or information any act or omission is charged against any person as an offence, and it is given in evidence on the trial of such person for that offence that he was insane, so as not to be responsible, according to law, for his actions at the time when the act was done or omission made, then, if it appears to the jury before whom such person is tried that he did the act or made the omission charged, but was insane as aforesaid at the time when he did or made the same, the jury shall return a special verdict that the accused is not guilty by reason of insanity.*[91]

Before considering whether the Defence have established insanity, the jury must be sure that the acts or omission that constitutes the criminal offence have been proven by the prosecution.

Where the defendant is found 'not guilty by reason of insanity' this is known as the 'special verdict.'[92] It is still the case that the issue of insanity is one to be decided by the jury. In reaching this verdict, they do not have to consider whether the prosecution have established the requisite state of mind of the Defendant at the time of the incident.

Where a special verdict is reached, the court must dispose of the defendant in one of the three ways set out in section 5 of the Criminal Procedure (Insanity) Act 1964.

---

[91] Section 2(1) of the Trial of Lunatics Act 1883

[92] Section 2(1) of the Trial of Lunatics Act 1883.

Evidencing Insanity

For a jury to return the special verdict of not guilty by reason of insanity, they must receive evidence in either written or oral form from two or more registered medical practitioners, at least one of whom is duly approved[93].

Appeal against a verdict of insanity from the Crown Court

Section 12 of the Criminal Appeal Act 1968 provides that where a person is subject to a verdict of not guilty by reason of insanity they may appeal that to the Court of Appeal with leave of the Court of Appeal or if the trial judge grants a certificate that the case is fit for appeal.

Where an appeal is allowed the Court of Appeal may replace the finding of not guilty by reason of insanity for a substantial guilty verdict to the offence and sentence accordingly, or acquit the Defendant.[94] Section 13(5) of the act provides that the Court of Appeal cannot substitute the finding of not guilty by reason of insanity with a sentence of death, but instead sentence to life imprisonment.

Section 6 of the act provides that the Court of Appeal on hearing an appeal against conviction, upon receiving evidence of two or more registered medical practitioners (of which one of whom is duly approved), and are of the opinion the proper verdict should have been one of not guilty by reason of insanity, can substitute the conviction for a verdict of not guilty by reason of insanity[95]. In those circumstances the Court of Appeal can go on to make a hospital order, supervision order or an absolute discharge[96]. In circumstances where the offence is fixed by

---

93 Section 1 of the Criminal Procedure (Insanity and Unfitness to Plead) Act 1991

94 Section 13 Criminal Appeal Act 1968

95 Section 6(1) Criminal Appeal Act 1968

96 Section 6(2) Criminal Appeal Act 1968

law (murder) the court shall make a hospital order with a restriction order.

The opposite approach lies in section 14 of the act, which allows the Court of Appeal to replace a verdict of not guilty, with a verdict of not guilty by reason of insanity, where they are satisfied the Defendant acted in the manner alleged (and upon hearing medical evidence from two practitioners at least one of which is approved) and was acting under a disability, as per M'Naghten, at the time.[97]

Insanity in a Magistrates' and Youth Court

Although there is no procedure for a special verdict, insanity is a common law defence which can be raised in a magistrates' court. If it is established, it prevents conviction.[98] The court may make a hospital order or a guardianship order by operation of section 37(3) of the Mental Health Act 1983. An appeal from the Magistrates' Court sentence of a hospital order or a guardianship order lies with the Crown Court.

---

97 Section 14(1) Criminal Appeal Act 1968

98 *R. (on the application of Singh) v Stratford Magistrates' Court* [2008] 1 Cr. App. R. 2; *R. v Horseferry Road Magistrates Court Ex p. K* [1997] Q.B. 23, [1996] 2 WLUK 217

CHAPTER SIX

THE UTILITY OF PSYCHIATRIC EVIDENCE IN ESTABLISHING SELF DEFENCE

In assessing whether a defendant has acted in self the defence the jury will need to consider whether they had used reasonable force in the circumstances. This considers two questions: first, was the use of force necessary in the circumstances which the defendant believed, and second if so was the force used reasonable in the circumstances.

The question of the circumstances which the Defendant believed they were in at the time force was used clearly involves a subjective assessment of their state of mind at the time of the incident. However an objective element is injected in assessing whether the force used was reasonable on the basis of the facts as the accused believed them. Would a reasonable person regard the force used as reasonable or excessive?[99]

In establishing whether the amount of force used by someone in self-defence is reasonable or not, it is not appropriate, save exceptional circumstances which would make the evidence especially probative, to take account of whether the defendant was suffering from some psychiatric condition.

In *R v Jason Canns*[100] the Court of Appeal was asked to consider whether it was appropriate to consider psychiatric evidence adduced by the

[99] R v Williams G 78 Cr App R 276 and R v Oatbridge 94 Cr App R 367

[100] [2005] EWCA Crim 2264

Appellant in relation to the reasons why they had killed a nurse whilst detained as an in-patient at a secure hospital.

The appellant, who suffered from paranoid schizophrenia, had killed a nurse whilst being detained as an in-patient at the hospital. The defence raised at trial was one of self-defence, namely that as a result of their delusional beliefs they considered the nurse had attacked the appellant with the intention of raping him. It was argued that the evidence of the Appellant's mental disorder was relevant to the issue of the reasonableness of the force used.

The court concluded that, save in exceptional circumstances, it was not appropriate when deciding whether reasonable force had been used or not to consider an individual's psychiatric condition. It is not for a defendant to set their own standard of reasonableness but a for a jury, when considering the circumstances other than the psychiatric condition, to set the standard of reasonableness in the case.

The Court of Appeal noted that each member of the court had found it impossible to identify the sort of exceptional circumstances in which it would be appropriate to take a psychiatric condition from which a defendant is suffering into account, when addressing the question of whether excessive force is used[101].

The court commended the summing up of the trial judge in rationalising why this was the case:

> *19. … Indeed, there is, in the course of the summing-up, at page 13F, a clear explanation by the trial judge of why the law is as it is:*
>
> *"Because when you think about it, it cannot be right that the more psychotic a defendant may be the greater his chances of acquittal, because of his genuine delusions. Do you follow? If the test was a purely subjective one through and through, why psychotic and dangerous defendants are likely always to be acquitted because their reaction was*

[101] Ibid at para 16

> *reasonable by their own standards. The law is that defendants do not set their own standards of reasonableness. It is not for a defendant in his own mind to set the standard of reasonableness, it is for the jury, considering all the circumstances but not the psychiatric condition, to set the standards of reasonableness in considering the individual case."*[102]

That reasoning, as supported in *Canns*, was further approved in *R v Seun Oye.*[103] The defendant was found in a staff changing area of Westfield Shopping Centre. The police were called by which point they had climbed into a void in the ceiling and proceeded to throw cutlery at officers. The defendant was subsequently arrested and taken into custody. Whilst in custody he punched an officer to the face and fractured the jaw of another.

Unchallenged psychiatric evidence was advanced at trial suggesting the defendant was insane at the time of the incident and both parties advanced submissions that the defendant should receive the special verdict. However the defence also raised the issue of self-defence. Despite repeating to the jury on no fewer than five occasions that the unchallenged expert evidence of two psychiatrists was that the defendant was insane at the time of the offence, the jury returned convictions on all counts.

On appeal the Court of Appeal raised the issue of self defence against the context of unchallenged evidence that the Appellant was insane at the time of the incident. The Court noted that it was argued by the Appellant:

> *44. … "in the circumstances as the defendant believed them to be, the prosecution could not, on the evidence, prove that the degree of force used was unreasonable or disproportionate in those circumstances. That his belief as to those circumstances derived from his insane*

[102] Ibid at para 19

[103] [2014] 1 Cr. App. R. 11

delusion, it was submitted, was immaterial. The point was that that was his genuine, if insanely deluded, belief.

45. If this is right, the potential implications for other cases are most disconcerting. It could mean that the more insanely deluded a person may be in using violence in purported self-defence the more likely that an entire acquittal may result. It could mean that such an individual who for his own benefit and protection may require hospital treatment or supervision gets none. It could mean that the public is exposed to possible further violence from an individual with a propensity for suffering insane delusions, without any intervening preventative remedies being available to the courts in the form of hospital or supervision orders. Thus, whatever the purist force in the argument, there are strong policy objections to the approach advocated on behalf of the defendant.

46. In our view, it is not right.

47. The position remains, as we think plain from the provisions of s.76 of the 2008 Act, that the second limb of self-defence does include an objective element by reference to reasonableness, even if there may also be a subjective element: see, in particular, s.76(6) and see also the decision in R. v Keane and McGrath [2010] EWCA Crim 2514. An insane person cannot set the standards of reasonableness as to the degree of force used by reference to his own insanity. In truth, it makes as little sense to talk of the reasonable lunatic as it did, in the context of cases on provocation, to talk of the reasonable glue-sniffer.[104]"

In assessing the reasonableness of the force used by a defendant an objective assessment by reference to the circumstances must take place. A person suffering from insanity cannot set the stand of reasonableness of the degree of force used by reference to their own insanity.

[104] Ibid at para 44 – 47

Whilst dismissing the appeal in respect of arguments advanced surrounding self-defence, the Court was at unease with the verdict of the jury in the context of the mutual position that the defendant was insane at the time of the incident, and as such should receive the special verdict. The Court could not see a rational basis for the jury's decision, and as such chose to interfere by substituting the conviction for the special verdict under s6 of the Criminal Appeal Act 1968.

In *R v Press and Thompson*[105] the court considered whether it was right to direct the jury to consider the Appellant's PTSD consequent to military service when considering the issue of self-defence and the reasonableness of the force used. This was a point, not raised by either party in the grounds of appeal, but by the Registrar. The Court made the following observations at paragraph 44

> *44. We emphasise it is common ground that it was not Dr Anderson's evidence in the present case that Thompson did hold or may have held a "deluded" belief that he needed to use force.* ***The essence of his evidence was that Thompson's condition may have caused him to react over-sensitively to perceived threat.*** *The issue that arose in the present case was not whether the appellant was acting under a psychotic or other delusion as to the nature of the threat he faced. It was whether, having perhaps mistakenly judged the need to use force at all (through the effects of PTSD), he then exceeded what was reasonable in the circumstances as he understood them to be. The Recorder correctly directed the jury that Dr Anderson's evidence was relevant to the question whether the appellant Thompson held a genuine belief that he was under a threat such as required him to use force. Further, the Recorder correctly left to the jury the question whether there was any room for a finding that Thompson had a genuine belief in the need to defend himself if they were sure that nothing had been said or done that could have caused even an oversensitive reaction.* ***As to the third question, whether the force used was reasonable in the circumstances, the Recorder correctly, in our view, invited the jury to consider the evidence of Dr Anderson when resolving the question***

105 [2013] EWCA Crim 1849

> ***whether Thompson did only what he believed was necessary in the circumstances.*** *The Recorder made clear, however, that it was for the jury, not the defendant, to resolve the ultimate question whether the degree of force used was reasonable. In these circumstances, we agree with the parties that there was no misdirection to the jury upon the issue of self-defence.*

The Court considered that the psychiatric evidence in this case, namely that an individual with PTSD may overreact to a perceived threat, could be used by the jury in their assessment of whether the force used by the Appellant was only that which was necessary in the circumstances.

Immediately prior to the above paragraph the Court of Appeal referred to the cases of *Canns* and *Oye* (both of which are referred to above). The court begins para 44 by observing that it was not the psychiatric evidence that the Appellant did hold or may have held a deluded belief (a common factor in both Canns and Oye). The Court sets out it was in fact the psychiatric evidence that an individual with PTSD may react over sensitively to a perceived threat. This appears to be sufficient to distinguish from *Canns* and *Oye*. Thompson was not act under a deluded belief and used force as a result of that deluded belief, but instead suffered from a psychiatric condition that caused him to overreact in the circumstances. As such, the Court of Appeal allowed that evidence to be used in assessing the reasonableness of the use of force.

CHAPTER SEVEN

DISPOSAL OF CASES INVOLVING ELEMENTS OF MENTAL HEALTH TREATMENT

October 2020 saw a new overarching guideline on the topic of sentencing offenders with mental disorders, developmental disorders or neurological impairments come into force[106]. The guideline is not offence specific, but instead provides an explanatory approach to the various options available to the court, whilst highlighting some of the factors the court will consider when assessing how best to dispose of a case where the offender has a mental health condition.

The consultation followed the Court of Appeal's decision in the conjoined appeals of R v Edwards and others[107] which undertook a review of how cases involving mental health disposals were being considered, in particular the applications of sections 37, 41 and 45A of the Mental Health Act 1983. The court in Edwards noted that even in cases where the offender suffered from a mental health condition, there remained two pillars of sentencing: rehabilitation and punishment. It acknowledged that whilst sentencing individuals with mental health conditions may be difficult, particularly in respect of assessing their overall culpability, in order to comply with the purpose of sentencing set out in section 57 of the Sentencing Act 2020, this was a task that needed to be conducted by the sentencing judge. But in doing so, the court could not be blind to section 63 of the Sentencing Act 2020 in respect of how

---

[106] Sentencing offenders with mental disorders, developmental disorders, or neurological impairments – Sentencing (sentencingcouncil.org.uk)

[107] [2018] EWCA Crim 595

to determine the seriousness of the offence. It was the seriousness of the offence, and in particular the culpability of an offender with a mental health condition, that was the root issue in the appeals of *Edwards and others*.

Sentencing youths with autism or other mental conditions was considered in *R v PS, CF and Abdi Hadir.*[108] The court made a series of observations about how mental health conditions can affect sentencing. A mental health condition may be relevant to an issue of culpability, and the individual's ability to make a reasoned decision, understanding the consequences of that decision. The mental health condition may equally be relevant to the type of sentence that is passed. Where a custodial sentence is considered necessary, the mental health consideration may impact the length of the sentence and whether it can be suspended. Mental health may also be relevant to the issue of dangerousness. In respect of any requirements attached to a community order/suspended sentence, or an ancillary order, mental health conditions ought to feed in to ensure the purpose of the sentence being sought to be achieved by the court is carried out and understood.

Procedural Direction

Criminal Procedure Rule ("CrimPR") 28.8 sets out the directions to be given by the court where a medical report is required for sentencing purposes. It applies where the court is considering a hospital order. The court must, *inter alia*, identify the issues about which the court is likely to need medical evidence and the applicable legislation; the nature of expertise required; set directions for the commission of the expert report, whether through the arrangements available with the NHS or otherwise; set a timetable to produce reports; and identify the people to whom a report should be supplied.

Criminal Practice Direction ("CPD") part VII 'R' (Sentencing) provides useful guidance as to instructing medical experts for sentence. Even where a report is commissioned at the instigation of the court, that should

[108] [2019] EWCA Crim 2286

not be viewed as a substitute for a report commissioned by the defence where medical evidence is material to the defence case.[109]

The practice directions suggest that the timetable set by the court should require:

(a) the convening of a hearing to consider the report no more than 6 – 8 weeks after the court makes its request;

(b) the prompt identification of an appropriate medical practitioner or practitioners, if not already identified by the court, and the despatch of a commission or commissions accordingly, within 2 business days of the court's decision to request a report;

(c) acknowledgement of a commission by its recipient, and acceptance or rejection of that commission, within 5 business days of its receipt;

(d) enquiries by court staff to confirm that the commission has been received, and to ascertain the action being taken in response, in the event that no acknowledgement is received within 10 business days of its despatch;

(e) delivery of the report within 5 weeks of the despatch of the commission;

(f) enquiries into progress by court staff in the event that no report is received within 5 weeks of the despatch of the commission[110].

Where a hearing to consider the expert report has been set, but the expert report is not in fact prepared in time, the court should be told in advance of the hearing. In that eventuality, it will rarely be appropriate to dispense

[109] See Criminal Practice Direction 2015 as amended October 2019 Division VII R.1.

[110] See Criminal Practice Direction 2015 as amended October 2019 Division VII R.6

with the hearing, but the hearing may well be conducted by live link or telephone.

In the magistrates' court, regard must be had to section 11 of the Powers of Criminal Courts (Sentencing) Act 2000 which limits the duration of each remand pending preparation of a report to 3 weeks where the defendant is in custody and 4 weeks where the defendant is on bail.[111]

Following on from a determination of unfitness to plead and a subsequent determination that the defendant has committed the act or omission with which he is charged, or indeed from reaching a special verdict of not guilty by reason of insanity, a further expert report may be required as to recommendation of sentence. A further interview of the defendant by the originally instructed psychiatrist, followed by an addendum report on sentence may be the preferable approach.

In respect of a sentence stemming from a finding of unfitness to plead, a court can only impose a hospital order where it is satisfied that the defendant is suffering from a mental disorder.[112] The diagnosis of a mental disorder, and recommendations as to its susceptibility to treatment, the options for treatment, and the anticipated length of treatment should all be covered in an expert report. An analysis of the extent to which proper treatment would reduce any risk of reoffending should also be covered.

If appointed, and where it is relevant, the court expert will address the dangerousness criterion. It may therefore be of assistance if the defence expert provides their own analysis of the dangerousness of the defendant.

A report should also address the expert's opinion as to sentence, insofar as it falls within their expertise. The issue of whether the offender could be managed effectively in the community (by way of a supervisory order) properly falls within their ambit. Further, where it is relevant in the case, the question of the appropriateness of a hospital order with or without a

[111] Powers of Criminal Courts (Sentencing) Act 2000, section 11(2).

[112] Mental Health Act 1983, section 37(2).

restriction order should be addressed. The effect that any of these disposals might have on his mental disorder should also be addressed.

Section 5 Criminal Procedure (Insanity) Act 1964

Where a person is 'unfit to plead' but findings are made that the person did the act or made the omission charged against them, the court must go on to deal with that person in one of the three ways listed under section 5(2) of the Criminal Procedure (Insanity) Act 1964. These are:

- A hospital order (with or without restriction);
- A supervision order; or
- An absolute discharge.

Those disposals also apply in cases where a Defendant has been found not guilty by reason of insanity.

Hospital Orders: Section 37 Mental Health Act 1983

A section 37 hospital order provides that where the defendant is convicted of an offence punishable by imprisonment, either in the Crown or magistrates' court, the court can impose an order that the Defendant must remain at a hospital until they are assessed as mentally sound to be released.

In order for the court to have the power to make a hospital order, it must have received the evidence of two medical practitioners and thereby be satisfied that the defendant is suffering from a mental disorder.[113] In practice these will likely be the same practitioners as have examined the defendant to make a determination of unfitness to plead/insanity (if these routes have been progressed). It remains the case that at least one medical practitioner must be an approved clinician in accordance with section 12(2) of the Mental Health Act 1983.

[113] Mental Health Act 1983, section 37(2).

Even where psychiatrists recommend a hospital order under s37 Mental Health Act the court remains under an obligation to carefully consider all the evidence to determine whether a hospital order is the most suitable disposal. In considering this question the court will consider the extent to which the offender needs treatment, the extent to which the offending is attributable to the mental disorder, the extent to which punishment is required, and the overall protection of the public.

An order under s37 cannot be made unless arrangements have been put in place for admission to hospital within 28 days of the order being made.

Whilst the suitability of a section 37 order is being investigated, the court has the option to make an interim hospital order under section 38 of the Mental Health Act 1983. This will occur where the court has not yet received the final opinion of the psychiatrists, but has received evidence from two registered medical practitioners that there is reason to suppose that the mental disorder is such that it may be appropriate for a final hospital order to be made. An interim hospital order cannot be in place for a period longer than 12 weeks, and requires renewal every 28 days upon the evidence of the clinician responsible for the defendant that the continuation of the order is necessary.

The order will initially last 6 months, but may be extended for a further 6 months by the clinician responsible for the patient's care. Following 12 months the order may be extended for 12-month periods by the responsible clinician.

A person may apply to the Mental Health Tribunal to bring about their discharge. This can be done following 6 months of the order, and every 12 months thereafter. That person should be discharged where the Tribunal is satisfied that they are no longer suffering from a mental disorder justifying their detention in hospital.[114]

[114] Mental Health Act 1983, section 72(1).

Upon discharge from a section 37 order (or 45A order) the patient will receive aftercare services from the local authority until they are satisfied the person concerned no longer requires such services[115].

Restriction Orders – section 41 Mental Health Act 1983

A hospital order may be imposed with or without a restriction order. Only the Crown Court may make a hospital order with a restriction order.[116] A magistrates' court has the power to commit to the Crown Court where it considers that a restriction order may be appropriate.[117]

A restriction order imposes indefinite detention against whom a hospital order is imposed. Following the entry into force of the Mental Health Act 2007, a restriction order may no longer be time limited.[118] The order will apply indefinitely until it is discharged by the Secretary of State for Justice, the patient's responsible clinician or hospital management with the Secretary of State's consent, or by the Mental Health Tribunal. The status of those subject to a restriction order is reviewed systematically by a clinician at intervals of not more than one year.[119]

In order for the court to have the power to impose a restriction order, it must be necessary to do so "for the protection of the public from serious harm."[120] The approach to this assessment is given by the case of *R. v Beulah Birch.*[121] The seriousness of the offence should not be conflated with the risk to the public of serious harm through future offending: a minor offence by a mentally disturbed and dangerous individual may

---

[115] Section 117 Mental Health Act 1983

[116] Mental Health Act 1983, section 41(1).

[117] Mental Health Act 1983, section 43.

[118] Mental Health Act 2007, section 40.

[119] Mental Health Act 1983, section 41(6).

[120] Mental Health Act 1983, section 41(1).

[121] [1989] 11 Cr App R (S) 202

justify passing a restriction order;[122] equally, a serious offence committed by someone evaluated as having a low risk of reoffending may mean that a simple hospital order is appropriate.[123]

Whilst a section 37 order requires the evidence of two practitioners, either presented in written or oral form, for a section 41 order oral evidence is required from at least one medical practitioner for the examination of the court. However, it is not a requirement for the evidence presented to have recommended a section 41 restriction order.

Where the person would have faced a sentence 'fixed by law' upon conviction and the court has the power to make a hospital order, the court must make a hospital order with a restriction order.[124] This is so irrespective of whether they would otherwise have had the power to make a restriction order. The only sentence fixed by law is a life sentence for murder.

Section 45A – Hospital and Limitation Orders (Hybrid Orders)

A section 45A order, known as a hybrid order, is a sentence that combines a custodial sentence with a hospital and limitation direction. Where the health of a patient subject to a section 45A order improves such that it will justify their release from hospital, the responsible clinician or tribunal will notify the Secretary of State to remit the patient to prison under s50(1) of the Mental Health Act 1983, to serve the rest of their sentence.

The Crown Court can pass a section 45A order where, having met the evidential requirements for a section 37 order with or without restrictions under section 41, the court additionally decides to impose a sentence of imprisonment in respect of the offence. In *Edwards; Knapper; Payne; Langley*[125] the court considered that the sentencing court should first

[122] See *Jones v Isleworth Crown Court* [2005] EWHC 662 (Admin).

[123] As was the case in *R v Birch*, as well as in the case of *Courtney* (1987) 9 Cr.App.R.(S.) 404.

[124] Criminal Procedure (Insanity) Act 1964, section 5(3).

[125] [2018] EWCA Crim 595

consider whether a hospital order may be appropriate under s37(2)(a), before then going on to consider whether a penal element under s45A of imprisonment was required. Where the court considers no such penal element is required, it should have sound reasons for that, which may include attribution of the offence was substantially due to the offender's illness[126]. The court noted that the more serious the offence, the higher the emphasis should be on public protection and therefore the need for a penal element to the sentence. This was noted further in *Fisher*[127] which stated that s37 and 41 orders do not involve elements of punishment, while s45A orders do carry a punitive element.

If during the period of the sentence passed by the Crown Court the patient's health sufficiently improves such that they no longer require detention in hospital they will be transferred to prison to serve the remainder of their sentence. At this point the hospital and limitation direction will cease to have effect.

If the automatic release date from custody passes (a period of time on home detention curfew does not apply for these purposes) without improvement in the patient's health the limitation direction falls away, but the patient will remain in hospital subject to an unrestricted hospital order. The consequence of this is that the decision to discharge is a matter for the clinicians, and not the Secretary of State.

Supervision Order

A supervision order requires a person to be supervised by a social worker, an officer of a local probation board or an officer of a provider of probation services for a period of no more than two years. The court will only make a supervision order if it is satisfied that it is the most suitable means of dealing with the accused, without the need for admission to hospital; that the identified supervising officer is willing to undertake the

[126] Ibid at para 12

[127] [2019] EWCA Crim 1066

period of supervision; and that arrangements have been made for the treatment specified in the order.[128]

It is not to be assumed that the supervising officer is willing to undertake supervision: there may well be very good reasons why a supervising officer is not willing, such as a lack of appropriate qualifications, and a failure to obtain consent could result in the supervision order being unlawful and therefore quashed.[129]

A supervision order may include a requirement that the supervised person submits to medical treatment, either for a part of the supervision period of for the whole period.[130] In order for that requirement to be imposed, it must be determined that, upon the advice of two or more registered medical practitioners, the supervised person requires and may be susceptible to treatment. The supervision order may also include a residence requirement.

Guardianship Order

Although a Guardianship Order is not available where a defendant is found unfit to plead in the Crown Court, it is available in the magistrates' court where the court has made a decision to dispose of the defendant without convicting them under section 37(3) of the Mental Health Act. A guardianship order can only be imposed on a defendant who is at least 16 years old. A person under a guardianship order is, generally, cared for in the community.[131] As the name of the order suggests, if confers powers on a person or authority named in the order in a guardianship role.[132] The powers that it confers on the guardian are:

[128] Criminal Procedure (Insanity) Act 1964, schedule 1A, para. 2.

[129] *City and County of Swansea v Swansea Crown Court* [2016] EWHC 1389 (Admin).

[130] Criminal Procedure (Insanity) Act 1964, schedule 1A, para. 4.

[131] See *R (on the Application of Paul Bukowicki) v Northamptonshire County Council* [2007] EWHC 310 (Admin), para. 8.

[132] Mental Health Act 1983, section 40(2).

- the power to require the patient to reside at a place specified by the authority or person named as guardian;
- the power to require the patient to attend at places and times so specified for the purpose of medical treatment, occupation, education or training;
- the power to require access to the patient to be given, at any place where the patient is residing, to any registered medical practitioner, approved mental health professional, or other person so specified.

The process by which a court will consider disposing with a case by way of guardianship order is explored in the case of *R (on the Application of Paul Bukowicki) v Northamptonshire County Council.*[133] The court must first have regard to section 37(2), where it must determine whether the offender is suffering from mental illness, psychopathic disorder, severe mental impairment or mental impairment and that the mental disorder he suffers from is of a nature or degree which warrants reception into guardianship. This decision mut be made with reference to the evidence of at least two registered medical practitioners. The court should also have regard to any information provided to it by the relevant local authority.[134]

The next stage is for the court to consider whether section 37(2)(b) of the Mental Health Act 1983 is satisfied: is it the case that, having regard to all the circumstances, a guardianship order is the most suitable way of disposing of the case. This must be read in conjunction with section 37(6), which makes it clear that the judge's decision to order

133 [2007] EWHC 310 (Admin)

134 *R (on the Application of Paul Bukowicki) v Northamptonshire County Council* [2007] EWHC 310 (Admin), para. 30.

guardianship can only be made if the local authority is content to receive the offender into guardianship.[135]

Following the making of a guardianship order, it may only be discharged upon application to the Mental Health tribunal by the nearest relative of the patient.

Mental Health Treatment Requirements

A Mental Health Treatment Requirement is an order that can be attached to either a suspended sentence or a community order. Where the court considers mental health treatment ought to be provided as part of a rehabilitative scheme, Schedule 9 section 16 of the Sentencing Act 2020 allows the court to attach a Mental Health Treatment Requirement. This provides that the offender must undertake treatment for a period of time specified by the court under the care of a registered medical practitioner or psychologist.

The treatment required as part of the order must consist of treatment either as a resident or non-resident patient in a care home or hospital, or treatment under the direction of a registered practitioner or psychologist.

In order to make a mental health treatment requirement the court must be satisfied that the offender may be susceptible to treatment, that does not warrant either a hospital or guardianship order, is willing to comply with the requirement, and that arrangements have or can been put in place for the treatment to be delivered.

The decision whether to make a mental health treatment requirement will fall within the discretion of the sentencing judge taking into account all the factors presented before them. That an individual suffers from mental health issues that would benefit from treatment is simply one matter to be considered. The sentencing court will bear in mind that

---

[135] *Ibid* at para. 31.

medication can be dispensed in a custodial setting, and that treatment is not exclusively received outside of custody.[136]

[136] R v Morgan [2014] EWCA Crim 2814

CHAPTER EIGHT

DIGITAL FORENSICS

Digital forensics is the process by which information is extracted from a digital system, converted into a form that can be considered, processed and interpreted for the purpose of either obtaining further intelligence or use as evidence in criminal proceedings. The modern world has developed a proliferation of digital technology all providing potential sources of evidence. The extraction, investigation and analysis of this material has provided new challenges for law enforcement agencies. The sheer quantity of material that can readily be obtained requires new techniques to analyse the material.

As technology develops so does the potentials for accessing digital information. No longer are we solely connected to the internet through a desktop PC. The greater use of smartphones, tablets and even televisions or smart technology in the home has led to the greater capture of data which potentially holds evidential value. Digital forensics can therefore be broken down into several different areas (albeit, given the changing nature of the technology the lines between these groupings will inevitably blur over time):

Computer forensics: the identification, preservation, collection, analysis and reporting on evidence found on computers, laptops, and storage media.

Network forensics: the monitoring, capture and storage of activities over networks to discover the source of security attacks.

Mobile device forensics: the recovery of electronic evidence from mobile phones, smartphones, SIM cards, game consoles and the like.

Digital Image Forensics: The extraction and analysis of digitally acquired photographic images to validate their authenticity through the recovery of metadate to establish an image's history.

Digital video/audio forensics: the collection and analysis of sound and video recordings, confirming whether a recording is original or tampered with.

But as digital technology increases so does the potential for cybercrime. Cyber-attacks become more problematic on individuals and businesses which can cause significant disruption to the network. Those attacks will often take the form of either hacking (where a user gains access to material stored on a networked system without authorisation) or denial of service (where the system links are overloaded resulting in the system crashing). The Computer Misuse Act 1990 legislates for offences such as unauthorised access to computer material.

The use of digital technology also opens new possibilities for fraud. Forensic document examiners no longer limit their work to the use of handwritten signatures. Individuals are increasingly using digital signatures, which in turn have created new opportunities for fraud. Documents can be scanned and digitally altered using optical character recognition software, at which point they can be printed and passed off as the original. As these possibilities continue to develop for those with sufficient knowledge and a propensity for criminal activity, the role of the digital forensic expert continues to gain prominence.

A (very brief) overview of digital forensic data and its transmission

Much like DNA which is comprised of a series of ATCG base pairs, digital documents are produced by a series of 0's and 1's known as its binary code. It is the combination of 0's and 1's, combined with a set of instructions commonly known as 'software' that makes up individual pieces of data. A document on a digital device is produced as an electronic file.

A computer network exists when two or more computers are connected either by cables or by a wireless connection, typically via a local area network (LAN). Whenever a computer connects to a website, data is transmitted. When an operating system is running data transmission occurs in the background. Consequently, when a suspect device is identified the loss of digital data will be at the forefront of the investigators mind. The transfer of data similarly works with smartphones – turning a mobile phone on commences the transmission of data. Turning the phone off will result in the transmission ending as the network signal is broken.

In relation to computers, the files on a computer will often be stored on the internal hard drive. Data can also be stored temporarily in the volatile memory (or RAM). When undertaking an examination of a computer's memory duplicate copies of the contents of the memory will be recovered by the digital forensics examiner to provide a clear and complete audit trail of any changes made. Timing is key with any device that can transmit data, due to their ability to do so at any point whilst the device is on, even if not directly operated. Files may be deleted remotely through networking. Whilst the deletion of a file breaks up the underlying clusters of stored data, means of pulling the clusters back together exist through the appropriate software. However, the creation of new clusters of data can result in overwriting existing clusters, meaning the quick extraction of data, during periods of potential transmission is key.

A more recent development providing challenges for investigators is the use of 'cloud networking'. This allows for documents to be accessible from a computer based in the UK, whilst being held in a foreign jurisdiction through servers based abroad. This has provided investigators with further challenges in being able to obtain this material.

Obtaining Digital Material

Before the process of extraction and analysis of data is conducted, first the data must find its way into the hands of law enforcement authorities. How that is done can vary depending on whether the data is located within the UK or abroad.

Obtaining Digital Material from within the UK

There are several ways in which the UK law enforcement authorities can obtain digital forensic material. It is outside the scope of this book to go through each in a significant amount of detail, but the below provides an overview of some of the powers of law enforcement agencies in obtaining digital forensic material.

Material obtained directly from a personal or business addresses of the UK will generally follow the issuance of a search warrant that lists the type and nature of the material sought to be seized (as opposed to being handed over voluntarily). Section 8 of the Police and Criminal Evidence Act 1984 provides the Magistrates' Court with the power to authorise a police constable to enter and seize property from an address where it is believed material of substantial evidential value to an indictable offence exists. Section 19 of the same act provides the constable with the power to seize anything on the premises where they have reasonable grounds to believe it is evidence in relation to an offence, and that it is necessary to seize the item. Section 20 provides that where information is held on a computer and therefore stored in electronic form, the officer can request to obtain a copy of it in a form that can be taken away. However, this section must be considered alongside sections 50 and 51 of the Criminal Justice and Police Act 2001 (seizure from premises and person respectively). These sections provide that where material that can lawfully be seized is formed as part of something else (for example, underlying computer files and data as part of a computer or social media messages on a mobile phone) the constable has the power to seize the whole of the item (the computer or the phone). The 2001 provisions remedy the position outlined in *Chesterfield Justices, ex parte Bramley*[137] which noted that under PACE there was no power to seize items for the purpose of sifting through the material at a later time.

Obtaining communications data, such as the type used to produce cell site reports, is sought under the Regulation of Investigatory Powers Act 2000 ('RIPA2000'). A person designated to make such a request can

[137] [2000] QB 576

obtain communications data from a communications operator where it is for the purpose of preventing or detecting crime.

Part 3 of RIPA2000 deals with obtaining pin and password protected electronic data. Section 49 provides that where protected information has come into the possession of law enforcement agencies a notice can be provided to a person believed to hold the key to the protected information imposing an obligation to disclose the key to the protected information. The effect of failing to comply with a section 49 notice, where it would otherwise be reasonably practicable to do so, is that a person commits a criminal offence under section 53 of the act. This offence provides the s49 notice procedure with some teeth.

Section 2 of the Criminal Justice Act 1987 authorises the Director of the SFO to issue a notice to a person whose affairs are to be investigated or any other person believed to hold relevant information, requiring them to answer questions or furnish information in relation to an investigation. Where there are reasonable grounds for non-compliance, a court may issue a warrant for non-compliance with the notice. Further, where a person fails to comply with the notice without reasonable excuse, they may be guilty of an offence[138].

Obtaining Digital Material from abroad

Further hurdles arise when the digital material is held abroad. However, the process was simplified with the introduction of the Crime (Overseas Production Orders) Act 2019 which received Royal Assent in February 2019. The introduction of the overseas production order allowed UK law enforcement agencies[139] to obtain electronic data directly from service providers that are based outside the UK. In order to obtain an Overseas Production Order an appropriate officer must apply to a Crown Court

---

[138] See for example a recent case of Anna Mackevitch, reported at https://www.sfo.gov.uk/2020/01/30/anna-machkevitch-found-guilty-of-failing-to-comply-with-a-section-2-notice/

[139] See section 2 of the Crime (Overseas Production Orders) Act 2019 for the full list of those entitled to apply for the order

judge to compel a company or individual to provide the electronic data stored outside the UK. An order requires the person against whom the order is made to either produce the electronic data in question or provide access to it. Electronic data is defined as data stored electronically, but the act excludes items that are subject to legal professional privilege and documents which amount to a confidential personal record[140] The grounds for making an order are set out at section 4 of the act. They outline that the judge hearing the application must be satisfied there are reasonable grounds for believing that the person against whom the order is sought:

- Operates or is based in a country outside the UK and which is subject to a designated international co-operation arrangement.

- That an indictable offence has been committed, and proceedings for the offence or an investigation has commenced, or that the investigation is in relation to terrorist activity.

- The person against whom the order is sought has possession or control of the electronic data specified.

- The data, in whole or in part, is likely to be of substantial value to the proceedings or investigation.

- The data is likely to be relevant evidence in respect of the proceedings or investigation.

- That it is in the public interest for the data to be produced or accessed.

Should an order be made, the contents should include the specific electronic data to be produced or accessed, the identity of the person who

[140] Defined in section 3(7) of the Crime (Overseas Production Orders) Act 2019 as a record concerning an individual's physical or mental health or counselling or assistance given and was created giving rise to an obligation of confidence.

is to receive the data, and the period by which the data should be provided/made accessible (no longer than 7 days from service of the order)[141]. Section 8 of the act provides that the order may include a non-disclosure requirement. The judge making the order may order that the party made subject to the order not disclose that the order exists, without the leave of the judge or the person making the application. This requirement to not disclose the existence of the order can continue even if the overseas production order is ultimately revoked.

The process was introduced following criticism with the previous process of mutual legal assistance which could notoriously take years to produce results. The process also fills a lacuna in the law highlighted in *R (on the application of KBR Inc) v Serious Fraud Office.*[142] In *KBR Inc* the Supreme Court ruled that a notice served under s2 Criminal Justice Act 1988 by the SFO requiring the production of sought material from the recipient of the section 2 notice could not be used to compel a foreign company which had no UK presence or business activity in the UK to produce documents held oversees.

Principles of Examination

Having obtained the digital forensic material it will be subject to examination. Whenever a piece of digital technology is recovered for examination that examination will be led by a series of key principles:

- When a device is turned on, there is the potential for data to change and new data to be downloaded or pre-existing data to be modified. There are ways in which this risk can be mitigated. In the case of mobile phones, for example, turning the phone into airplane mode or the use of a Faraday bag prevents the transmission of data.

[141] Section 5 of the Crime (Overseas Production Orders) Act 2019

[142] Initially in the High Court at [2018] EWHC 2368 (Admin) and later in the Supreme Court at [2021] UKSC 2

- Where data is accessed it must be performed by a person competent to do so. Actions, which have the potential to change data must be explained for their relevance and implications.

- Any action must be audited. An audit trail or record of all processes and actions applied to the digital evidence should be kept. The audit trail should be in sufficient detail such that a third party can review those notes and understand how and why actions have been taken.

- The person in charge of the investigation will have overall responsibility for ensuring that the law and these principles are adhered to.

These are derived from the ACPO Good Practice Guide for Digital Evidence and are repeated in the AG Guidelines on Disclosure[143]. They remain the foundation for the conduct of any examination of digital forensic material. They highlight the importance of continuity and integrity when dealing with digital forensic evidence, with case ownership required to ensure these principles are applied. Where there is the possibility for data to change without the direct input or knowledge of the examiner, preservation of the original data to allow for an objective assessment of the evidence in court is vital.

Examination of Crime Scenes and Recovery of Evidence

A crime scene may include many different data storage devices or media. They can provide a valuable source of evidence. The most common sources of storage devices are PCs/laptops, and mobile phones. Where a computer is located at a crime scene, examiners will photograph the scene, including the position of any leads which may facilitate data transmission. If off, computers will not be turned on for the same reason. Power sources will be removed to prevent accidental activation of the item, thereby commencing data transmission. A search ought to be conducted of the local area for notebooks/notes which may contain

[143] See Annex A on Digital Disclosure of the AG Guidelines

passwords and/or usernames. Where a computer is switched on, the individual using the computer may be spoken to about the setup of the system, including confirming any passwords. Turning off live systems without shutting them down correctly may result in data being lost. When appropriate the hardware will be seized. The essential principle behind a structured and careful withdrawal of the hardware is to ensure evidence on the hard disk is unchanged. The aim will be to produce an image of the memory of the device exactly as it was when the item was seized.

In respect of a mobile phone the immediate step will be to isolate the device from the network. This can be achieved by, for example, turning the device off at the point of seizure (although passwords may then be required to regain access) or placing the device in a shielded bag. Manual examination can be recorded to ensure an audit trail of the steps taken to avoid any concern over data loss. An examination strategy should be established, which is appropriate to the nature of the case. At a basic level standard forensic tools can extract active data from both the handset and the SIM. At an intermediate level a flash dump may be able to recover deleted data. At an advanced level the removal of memory chips is possible, retrieving deleted handset data.

Having taken possession of the relevant hardware the investigation process can commence. Whilst the investigation process will almost certainly vary according to the necessities of an individual case the examination process is likely to comprise several stages:

- Recovery – data is extracted, which will involve, for example, making a copy of the hard disk of a computer, downloading data from a mobile phone, or recovering data from a remote system. The data is then processed to allow it to be analysed. This may involve decrypting the data or recovering deleted files.

- Collection – having recovered and extracted the complete set of data from the systems, it will be searched to find evidence of relevance.

- Examination and Analysis – data is analysed and interpreted by the expert. The process will explain the origin and significance of the evidence. The probative value of the evidence will be assessed. This process will vary depending on the nature of the case in hand. For example, a case of possession of indecent images will consider where on the system the indecent images were found, when they were created, when they were last accessed and the file structure in which the images were located amongst other matters.

- Presentation – the findings of the analysis are communicated, potentially in the form of a written report which can be presented as evidence in court.

Once the information is recovered it must be assessed and reported on in the form of a statement or expert evidence. In most cases it will not simply be a requirement to show that the data was present, but that the Defendant was aware of the data and accessed it. This knowledge can be ascertained by examination of recent file history, browsing history, or passwords associated with file encryption for example. Reviews of this information may lend support to the proposition that the Defendant was aware of the existence and contents of the file on their device. Another consideration often raised is how the file was obtained – was it obtained purposefully or accidentally? Is it possible the user's system was hacked or downloaded bundles of data without knowing the full extent of what was being downloaded?

Disclosure

Digital forensic material has produced difficulties with the disclosure process. With laptop computers routinely holding 128, 256 or more gigabytes of data the paper equivalent is massive. As an illustration 27 gigabytes of data, if printed out on A4 paper would create a stack of paper 920 metres high.

Whilst ordinarily material must be examined in detail by the disclosure officer, in respect of digital material it may be appropriate to examine digital material by using software search tools. The AG's guidance on disclosure of digital material recommends a record be kept of all digital material seized and retained, and a strategy developed to identify how material will be analysed. The record should include details of who carried out the process, as well as the date and time of work carried out.[144] A record of search terms should be maintained as well as a log of key decisions made in respect of the search for material on digital devices.

Even where material is not examined in detail it must be appropriately described on the schedule of unused material. The extent of the examination, and how that was conducted, must also be described, together with any justification or how the approach was taken. Generally, this will take the form of a disclosure management document.

The service of the disclosure management document may produce other reasonable lines of enquiry, as may the service of a defence statement. Upon receipt of these, the disclosure officer has a further duty to undertake any further reasonable lines of enquiry.

Challenges in extracting the digital evidence

Whilst digital evidence provides greater opportunities for law enforcement agencies to obtain inherently more personal evidence for use in criminal proceedings it comes with its own challenges. The underlying data required is not always readily available. The data could be encrypted or stored in the cloud which can make access difficult. Encryption tools, to protect data, are more readily available and provide increased levels of security of data. The original information will be encoded using an encryption key and algorithm. A corresponding key and algorithm are then needed to decrypt the data. It is possible to not only encrypt stored data, but also whole devices and online communications, such as emails and instant messaging services. End to end encryption is becoming a more popular means of encryption to prevent interception of messages.

[144] AG Guidelines on Disclosure, Annex A digital material

Furthermore, increased use of cloud computing (involving online access to data storage) presents a challenge to digital forensic practitioners. Data can quickly change and be overwritten from multiple sites. The result can be the loss of data which can make independent verification at a later date difficult. Password protection on cloud storage can also slow down access to the data.

Serious criminal activity can put in place measures to prevent forensic investigation. Changing the dates and times of files can prevent the construction of a reliable timeline. Overwriting file can permanently destroy the original material. Partitioning digital storage with multiple passwords that lead to different sections of the drive, some with incriminating materials, and others without can slow progress with any investigation.

Finally, the rapid pace of technological change can present problems. New systems and applications must be studied to understand how they operate and how reliable evidence can be extracted. This results in investigators playing 'catch-up'. The volume of data that can now be stored on devices is such that processing it can take a long time. The use of search tools and parameters to focus searches can assist in ensuring compliance with the prosecutor's disclosure obligations.

CHAPTER NINE

CELL SITE EVIDENCE

When the user of a mobile phone makes a call, sends a text message, or sends or receives data over the internet, it communicates with ground-based equipment through a two-way link. The mobile handset is effectively a computer with a two-way radio. As the user moves around during the communication the connection with the ground-based equipment may change to ensure continuity in quality of the connection. These pieces of equipment are called cells, hence the name cellular telephone.

When a mobile (cellular) telephone is used the network provider used at that particular moment to facilitate the communication (through a sim card) creates a record of the activity. That record will include information such as the time and date of the activity, the type of activity, and the cell mast involved in facilitating that communication. It is the examination of those call data records and the analysis of the cell that allow experts to attempt to determine the location of a telephone at a particular time of use.

Definitions

There are very often a common set of technical terms used in this type of evidence outlined below:

Subscriber Identity Module ('SIM'): Commonly known as a sim card, this device stores the International Mobile Subscriber Identity number. A sim card can be moved between different mobile phones, meaning multiple sim cards can be used with a mobile phone during a period of time ('sim swap').

International Mobile Subscriber Identity Number ('IMSI'): The IMSI number is a unique number that identifies a user on the mobile phone network. This number is stored on a SIM card.

Mobile Station International Subscriber Directory Number (MSISDN): The number used to dial in order to connect to a mobile phone with the associated SIM card (IMSI) linked number.

International Mobile Equipment Identity ('IMEI'): The IMEI is a unique number allocated to a mobile device, and can be used by a network to identify if a device is connected to the particular network. The IMEI is 15 digits comprising 14 digits and a check digit which is the last digit. This can be used to establish the origin, model and serial number of that handset. When used with the IMSI number it is possible to establish which mobile phone the SIM card was placed in at a particular time. When a device connects to a network the IMSI, MSISDN and IMEI are all recorded.

Call Detail/Data Records CDRs: When a mobile phone is used the network provider creates and stores a record of it in a Call Detail Record or Call Data Record or CDR. Different networks operators store different amounts of data in the CDRs. But they all include the type of call, date, time, duration, who called who, IMEI, first cell ID used, and last cell ID used.

Call data retention: Since October 2007 onwards the UK networks are required to store call records for calls/SMS/GPRS originating in the UK for 12 months.

Voice Call: An audio communication between different telephone devices. Voice Call Data Records are created at the time the voice call is answered. The calling network and the called network each create a matching CDR. For this reason, when assessing compiled call data records practitioners should be aware of the possibility of duplicate entries (one from the outgoing record, and one from the incoming record). Often this will be obvious and should be removed by analysis software by the examiner before service of any compiled schedules for presentation to the trier of fact. However, these entries can fall through the gaps with the result that traffic between two numbers appears heavier than what it is.

Short Message Service ('SMS'): Sent text messages are time and date stamped the moment they are sent to the network and a CDR created. When an SMS is delivered another CDR is created. Multimedia messages ('MMS') – images – create CDRs in a similar manner to SMS.

General Packet Radio Service ('GPRS'): Is used by mobile phones for data services including the internet, email, and instant messaging. Whilst a record will be made of the connection, it will not note the form of that connection, for example whether it constitutes the receipt or sending of an email or connection to a social media or other form of application. GPRS records can be created without any action by the phone user, for example the receipt of a late-night email or an overnight update of an application. GPRS Call Detail Records only show a start cell ID.

Call forwarding: Call forwarding (call diversion) of an incoming call to voicemail or another phone number can occur in several circumstances, including when the phone is switched off, not answered or engaged on another call. In these circumstances a call data record will be kept, but a cell ID may not be.

Cell sites and cell IDs

Each network operator has built their own network of radio transmitter and receivers across the United Kingdom, called cell sites. A cell site is the location where one or more cell ID's are based. A cell site can have multiple antenna each with its own ID. Each operator has built its own network of ground-based cell sites across the UK. These can be seen in fields, on buildings and can be stand-alone posts in towns or on shopping centres. The cell infrastructure will often be updated to keep up with changes and developments in technology meaning that the infrastructure in place at the time of a particular incident may not be the same when it is assessed for the purposes of criminal proceedings many months, if not years, later.

Cell sectors and azimuths

A typical cell site will use three or more cell sectors mounted on the same mast to ensure a full 360° service coverage. Cell antennae will commonly be stacked one above another, all pointing in the same direction. Overlaid cells may use the same or different technology (a 5G cell stacked on top of a 4G cell, on top of a 3G cell).

The range of the cell can dramatically vary depending on the location of the cell and the nature of the surrounding area. To determine the actual range of a cell requires a field survey be undertaken.

Adjacent cells provide overlapping coverage so that in principle no matter where you are located several cells can provide service. Away from built-up areas coverage becomes less, and in particularly rural areas there may be poor or no coverage at all. Away from conurbations cell sites are often found along major transit routes to ensure coverage along these journeys. In areas of poor service coverage within a city, lower powered street-level micro cells can be used to fill the gaps in the coverage.

Most cell IDs provide service in a particular direction. By using several cells on the same mast set at different angles an entire area can be covered.

A mobile phone might not use the cell nearest to it. The following is a non-exhaustive list of reasons why the cell utilised may not be the nearest:

- If a cell further away can provide better signal quality,
- If the nearest cell is already filled to capacity with ongoing calls,
- If the nearest cell is out of service for maintenance.

That this took place will not be noted on the call data records.

How can this technology be used in the criminal justice process?

The analysis of call data records is commonly used to assist establish the use, location, and movement of a mobile phone and its associated IMSI.

The records can establish proximity to the location of an alleged offence or assist or undermine an alibi away from the relevant location. Where multiple phone data records are analysed the records can be used to infer relationships between phones.

In order to demonstrate that two mobile telephones are not together one must demonstrate that the physical distance between the cells used by the two phones is sufficiently great that, in the time period between communications, the mobile telephones could not have moved from the service area of one cell to the service area of another. If this criterion is met, then the demonstration is conclusive. That is the task of a cell site expert.

Cell Site Expert v Crime Analyst

The use of cell site expert evidence in criminal proceedings is often a three-stage process. Firstly, the call data records will need to be obtained from the network provider, through the police SPOC (single point of contact). Once obtained that data will be mapped. Cell site locations can be readily established, and these can be noted on a map alongside the location of the alleged criminal activity. Finally, that map will be interpreted – what is the range of the particular cell, what is the relevance of the cell mast, etc. It is the act of interpretation that requires a cell site expert and beyond the role of a crime analyst.

In recent years, it is of growing prevalence that prosecuting authorities will attempt to rely on crime data analysts (those that plot the locations of the cell site against the location of the alleged crime) incorrectly believing they are doing the job of an expert. This should be avoided. A crime data analyst can tell a trier of fact that a particular cell was connected at a particular time and date – that this means the phone was within a few hundred metres of the cell rather than a few hundred miles (which will often be the point the prosecuting authority are seeking to make) falls within the ambit of the expert and not the analyst. It is an act of interpretation and analysis of the map, based upon technical knowledge and assessment of cell technology which leads to the conclusion in evidence that the prosecuting authority will need – i.e. an expert's assessment.

What can an expert do?

The role of a cell site expert will be to consider whether a mobile telephone can be placed in a particular area at a particular time. To do this several examinations can be undertaken.

A field survey is undertaken to determine which cell IDs can provide service at a location or in an area or along a route. A mobile phone running engineering software or other specialised network monitoring equipment is used to monitor and log data from the nearby cell IDs.

The field survey reflects the state of the network at the time of the survey. The underlying assumption of any cell site analysis is that the network configuration is the same as when the calls were made, or that any changes in technology or usage are minor or negligible in their effect.

A spot survey can be carried out around a single location (usually an address) to determine what cell ID's can provide service to that location.

A survey along a route can be performed by travelling a predetermined route whilst simultaneously checking cell coverage to establish what cells can be connected during a journey. The analysis can be used to support or undermine a case theory involving alibi.

Challenging a Cell Site Expert

Cell site analysis alone cannot alone prove precisely where a mobile phone was at a particular time. The phone must have been located with the service area of that cell, the size of which can be determined by several different things. Cell site analysis can be used to eliminate a location: for example if a suspect states they were at home when a phone call occurred the home address can be surveyed to establish whether a particular cell ID can be connected to at that location.

Furthermore, it is quite possible that the network hardware infrastructure or software has changed (new cells installed, cells removed, antennas orientated differently etc.) since the day of the communication in question. Consequently, analysis at a later date may have increased the geographic area of coverage since the original communication. Equally the network telephone traffic at the time a call was routed, which could have resulted in the communication moving to a different cell, cannot be replicated.

Cell site analysis cannot determine who was using a mobile phone during a call, i.e. whether the registered owner or attributed handler of the phone was making the call, or that it was in the use of another. The call data records cannot establish the content of the telephone call or SMS message (a telephone mobile download may include saved SMS messages).

CHAPTER TEN

MODERN SLAVERY

The past few years have seen an increase in the recognition of individuals vulnerabilities as potential modern-day slaves. Practitioners should have at the forefront of their mind not just questions about what happened, but why something happened.

This greater recognition has been reflected in the upsurge of cases before the Court of Appeal assessing historic matters where questions surrounding why an individual committed an offence was not asked, or if they were the relevance and significance of the answers was not spotted.

This chapter does not focus on the appeal element of the slavery defence, but instead how an expert can assist in develop and advance an individual seeking to rely upon the defence at first instance.

Section 45 Modern Slavery Act 2015

2015 saw the formalisation of the modern slavery defence. The defence varies between whether or not an individual has reached the age of 18 at the time of committing the act which constitutes the offence.

A person aged 18 or over benefits from the defence if they do the act because they are compelled to do so, the compulsion is attributable to slavery or relevant exploitation, and a reasonable person in the same situation as the person having the person's relevant characteristics would have no realistic alternative to doing that act.

A person under the age of 18 benefits from the defence if they do the act as a direct consequences of the person being a victim of slavery or relevant exploitation, and a reasonable person in the same situation as the person having the person's relevant characteristics would do the act.

In advancing the defence a number of experts may be of use: a psychiatrist and/or psychologist to assess the person's relevant characteristics – are they easily led? Do they have an unusually low level of intelligence? Do they suffer from a mental health disorder which affects their relationships with others, their level of trust, or an understanding of what is happening to them? These are all questions that an appropriate expert can report on.

However recent years have seen a rise in experts addressing trends in modern slavery. The support of an expert who specialises in this area can be of great utility when presenting a case, or seeking to persuade the prosecution not to proceed with the case.

Who is and isn't an expert?

The question of who is and isn't an expert in matters of modern slavery was subject to scrutiny in the 2021 case *R v Kevin Brecani.* The Court of Appeal, in a decision handed down by the Lord Chief, gave consideration as to whether the decision of a caseworker appointed by the Single Competent Authority under the National Referral Mechanism was admissible in criminal proceedings.

Practitioners will be aware that an individual who raises the issue of slavery, or who are believed to be victims of slavery (even if they are not aware themselves of that potential status), should be referred to the NRM (National Referral Mechanism) so that the relevant competent authority can give consideration to the individual's circumstances.

The number of referrals has increased in recent years. In 2014 there were 2,340 referrals. In 2020 that number had exceeded 10,000[145].

Following referral an individual will be spoken to about their experiences. They should be offered support whilst their case is considered in respect of the provision of legal advice, accommodation and emotional and wellbeing support.

[145] 2021 UK Annual Report on Modern Slavery: 2021 UK Annual Report on Modern Slavery (accessible version) – GOV.UK (www.gov.uk)

The Single Competent Authority will make an initial or 'reasonable grounds' decision. Following receipt of further information, usually an interview with the individual subject of the referral, a 'conclusive grounds' decision will be made. This decision is made on the balance of probability, i.e is it more likely than not that they are a victim of modern slavery. This of course differs from the criminal standard of proof.

The government's 2021 annual report on modern slavery provides some insight into decision making. It reports that in 2020 89% of conclusive grounds decisions came back positive (with 92% of reasonable grounds decisions returning positive results). It notes the average time taken from referral to a conclusive ground's decision in 2020 was 339 days. That length of time will be of no surprise to practitioners familiar with the issues that arise a lengthy delay in reaching a conclusive grounds decision. As was noted in *Brecani* the CPS will ordinarily wait to know the outcome of a referral to the Competent Authority before deciding whether to continue proceedings (albeit the Crown are not bound by the decision).

The status of the NRM decision

The court in *Brecani* grappled with the issue of what use could be made of that decision in a criminal trial. The court reviewed the Single Competent Authority report against the requirements for expert reports under Criminal Procedure Rule part 19, noting an absence of much of the required information. Further in relation to case workers generally assigned by the Competent Authority there was no information available to the court to determine whether and in what area the case worker may be an expert. Case workers appeared to perform an administrative function in making the reasonable and conclusive grounds decision as opposed to an expert determination. The court departed from an earlier decision of *DPP v M*[146] which concluded that case workers were experts in human trafficking or modern slavery.

---

146 [2020] EWHC 344 (Admin)

The inadmissibility of the authority's decision at a criminal trial was reaffirmed in the subsequent decision of R v AAD and others [2022] 1 WLR 4042.

However, importantly, the court in both AAD and Brecani noted that it was clearly correct that a suitably qualified expert might be able to give evidence relevant to the questions that arise under the 2015 Act which are outside the knowledge of the jury.

How can an expert assist advance a defence of modern slavery?

The answer to this question is one that will be subject to ongoing discussion. It will be assessed on a case-by-case basis depending on the particular circumstances of the individual defendant and context in which it is suggested they became a modern slave.

One thing however is very clear: an expert cannot give evidence on the credibility of an individual's account of them being a slave. This is a matter wholly within the role of the trier of fact. It is entirely consistent with long running themes on expert evidence which are assessed elsewhere in this book.

The case of *R v AAD*[147] gave passing consideration as to the admissibility of expert evidence on questions relating to trafficking and exploitation. This was in the context of conjoined appeals of Appellants who advanced they had failed to be recognised as victims of trafficking at the time of the offence. Clearly this context is of significance to those advancing the section 45 defence.

The court in AAD were involved to explain the references in *Brecani* to societal and contextual factors on which expert evidence may be received. The court considered that it did not matter that members of a jury had not shared the experiences of defendants in human trafficking or modern slavery cases. It drew comfort from the fact that this principle applies in all criminal trials regardless of the nature of the charge, noting that few

[147] [2022] EWCA Crim 106

jurors for example will have been subjected to duress leading to participation in an armed robbery or found themselves in a riot. The court noted that the lack of first-hand experience of the circumstances does not require a witness to express a view on the consistency of how someone would behave it they found themselves under duress or caught up in a riot – these were matters that the jury would be well versed to consider applying their own experiences in life and draw conclusions.

The court expressly rejected submissions that an expert could give evidence on the vulnerability of a defendant and whether a set of facts met the definition of trafficking (or therefore slavery). This is consistent with English law been within the expertise of the court and requiring no further explanation. Further it was also considered consistent with, for example, an expert allowing to comment on factual assertions relating to the secondary transfer of DNA because in the absence of such commentary an expert couldn't give relevant evidence.

However the court did go on to state that there can be discrete issues in cases that properly require explanation by way of expert evidence, for example a defendants psychiatric or psychological state, or detail surrounding how gangs operate. However in order to give such evidence the court reminded practitioners that the expert evidence must be relevant to a matter in issue, the witness must be competent, and is the information outside of the court's own knowledge and experience.

For now the court appears to have made clear that expert evidence in relation to societal and contextual factors is to be welcomed – what exactly those societal and contextual factors are, will depend on a case by case basis, with matters been within the courts knowledge, and those outside been a fine line.

CHAPTER ELEVEN

GANGS, LYRICS AND ASSOCIATION

The use of evidence of gang association and music lyrics has come under scrutiny in recent years and its utility remains a controversial topic. Inevitably the term 'gang' can evoke emotions, stereotypes and prejudices in triers of fact. Imaginations can start to run wild, and perceptions of what gang membership involves and entails may start to overshadow reality.

Evidence related to gang association may be introduced as bad character under the Criminal Justice Act 2003. Its particular gateway will be fact dependent but most likely will be adduced either as important explanatory evidence under 101(1)(c) or relevant to an important matter in issue under section 101(1)(d).

Admissibility of Gang Association Material

The admissibility of gang related evidence has been given significant scrutiny over the past decade.

In *R v Elliott*[148] the Crown sought to adduce evidence in the form of letters written by the Appellant from when he was a serving prisoner demonstrating gang affiliation. A Detective Constable was called to give evidence to address issues surrounding gang membership around South London and the activities of the gangs of relevance. The Court of Appeal held that evidence of the gang's dress, pose and actions went directly to the issues that the jury had to determine and consequently were

[148] [2010] EWCA Crim 2378

admissible. It was right to leave the jury to assess the weight to the given to the evidence.

Later on in *R v Lewis*[149] evidence of gang affiliation was held to be admissible under section 101(1)(d) of the Criminal Justice Act 2003 in order to establish association with groups that were rioting across England in August 2011. Evidence of association was adduced in order to establish the issues of common purpose, identification, and whether the Appellants had been at the scene inadvertently or innocently. The Court noted that in cases of this type the issues a judge had to consider before adducing evidence of gang affiliation were – was it relevant to an important matter in issue between a defendant and the prosecution, was proper evidence to be adduced of the existence and nature of the gang, and was proper evidence showing that the defendant was a member or associated with the gang available? Consideration should also be given as to whether it would have such an adverse effect on the fairness of the trial that it ought to be excluded. In this case video evidence, along with police officer's expertise of the gangs was admissible.

The Privy Council gave guidance on the admissibility of evidence about the existence and practice of gangs in *Myers v The Queen.*[150] The Appellants in Myers were convicted of their involvement in a deliberating shootings of rival gang members. The incident was alleged to be a reprisal attack on opposing gang members. Evidence of gang association formed parts of the case against each of the Appellants, either as part of the prosecution case or in response to evidence adduced in cross examination of a prosecution witness. The gang association evidence went to the issue that the defendants had a motive to kill. The nature of the evidence was given by a police officer.

The Privy Council grappled with a number of issues, including the admissibility of gang evidence, and if admissible whether a police officer can give such evidence. Going back to basic principles the Committee considered that evidence was not admissible unless it was relevant, i.e.

---

149 [2014] EWCA Crim 48

150 [2016] UKPC 40

contributing something to the resolution of one or more of the issues in the case. Even if relevant, that does not automatically make it admissible. A route for admissibility must be identified. The Committee noted that even relevant and admissible evidence may be excluded if its prejudicial effect exceeded its probative value.

In *Myers* the Committee considered that the gang evidence went to the issue of identity which was the core issue in dispute. It showed that the defendants had a motive to kill the victims and were members of a group who were likely to feel aggrieved, and responded accordingly, to events shortly before the shooting.

It was held that gang evidence could be admissible, but will depend on the particular case and what legitimate role the evidence has in helping the jury to resolve one or more of the issues in the case. The Committee were not prepared to set down general rules for gang evidence beyond that proposition. The Court then went on to consider the issue of police officers as expert witnesses.

<u>The use of police officers as expert witness in cases of gang association</u>

Upon the admissibility of the principle of evidence relating to gangs and association been establish, consideration must then turn as to the form such evidence takes. As indicated in the cases reviewed above it is common practice for a police officer with knowledge of gangs local to the aera in which they operate to give this evidence. However, as with other experts, before admissible evidence can be advanced the officer must set out how they have obtained the expertise they profess to advance.

In *Elliot*[151] the applicant sought to argue that his conviction was unsafe because the judge was wrong to admit, as evidence of his bad character under s.101(1)(d) of the Act, evidence relating to his purported membership of a violent street gang. In accepting that evidence purporting to show the applicant's membership of a gang was admissible as bad character, the Court of Appeal went on to consider the issue of

151 [2010] EWCA Crim 2378

expertise. A Detective Constable with experience of the gangs operating in Peckham, as well as their involvement in drug and gun crime was called to give evidence. The Court held that:

> *"He was an officer with considerable experience of the violent criminal gangs of areas of south London including Peckham. The judge was entitled, in accordance with the principles stated by this court in R v Hodges [2003] 2 Cr App R 15, to permit that experienced police officer to give evidence based on his own experience and knowledge about the existence of the gangs and about the insignia of the gangs."*[152]

Hodges was a case in which the Court of Appeal held that the evidence of a police officer on the customary practice of drug users had been properly admitted due to the officer's substantial experience in relation to drug matters.

Similarly in *R v Lewis*[153] the Court of Appeal in considering evidence of gang affiliation to assist the jury in deciding whether an accused was present at the scene of a riot involving possession of firearms and arson commented as follows on the officer's relevant expertise:

> *"...to the second question, namely the sufficiency of proper evidence of the existence and nature of the gang or gangs, at the first trial, there was evidence was from officers from the Multi-Agency Gang Unit and the West Midland Police 'Gang Taskforce'. The officers had over a number of years dealt with the activities of street and criminal gangs in the Birmingham area. They had accumulated such experience and knowledge of the gangs as to be entitled to give evidence of the existence and operation of various gangs and about relevant signs and insignia associated with them.*
>
> *89. In the second trial, however, it was argued on behalf of Laing and Gray that DC Nevin who was to give the evidence, did not have the*

---

152 Ibid at para 11

153 [2014] EWCA Crim 48

requisite knowledge and experience. Mr Bartfeld pursued similar argument on behalf of Gray before us.

90. In a detailed ruling, the judge set out what DC Nevin had said at the first trial about his experience and knowledge. In summary, this was that, from 2006, he had been a police officer in the Newtown and Aston area just north of central Birmingham; and on the beat, he had come to understand the gang culture that existed there, partly from what he observed, and partly from what he heard from others. Then he moved to the Multi-Agency Gang Unit, set up in 2008, in which he worked with other police officers, the Youth Offending team, the Probation Service and other agencies. The purpose of the Unit was to try to persuade people who had some kind of affiliation with gangs to turn away from them. In the period 2008 to 2011, he spoke to many people in the Unit and with those affiliated to gangs. He learnt about the gangs, what they did, and what their signs were. He learned that some of the gangs produced videos. He knew about, or learned about, some of the crimes in which the gangs had been involved. The judge set out in detail what he said about each gang and affiliated gang[154].

The Court at para 94 of the Judgement noted that DC Nevin would, in talking to ex-gang members and other unidentified sources, be relying on hearsay. But it further noted that this had also been plainly the case in *Hodges*:

"In the present case, DC Nevin's evidence came in part from his own observation; in part, from other cases with which he had had involvement; in part, from what he had been told by ex-gang members or current gang members; and it also came from his discussions with colleagues in the Unit. The judge said:

'Now it is true that DC Nevin is relying in part on hearsay. True it is that he is relying on sources which are unidentified, but the same plainly applied in the case of Hodges, and plainly applies in many cases heard up and down the country about drug suppliers, and it plainly

---

[154] Ibid at para 88-90

must have applied to Mr Whiteway who was talking about gangs in south London.'"

It concluded at [95] that:

> *"the judge was entitled to conclude that this evidence came within the same ambit of evidence considered in Hodges and in Elliott and was admissible and that DC Nevin clearly had the requisite knowledge and experience."*

Following *Lewis* came the decision of the Judicial Committee of the Privy Council in *Myers v The Queen.*[155] As set out above the Committee in *Myers* considered three appeals against conviction. Each of the cases concerned a deliberate shooting. In each case the prosecution introduced evidence of the defendant's connection with gangs (the 'gang evidence').

The principal gang evidence at each trial was given by the same police officer. The issues on appeal went to the admissibility of the gang evidence, and, if it was considered admissible, whether it could be given by a police officer who had made a special study of the gangs concerned, as well as of gang culture generally.

On whether a police officer could act as expert witness on gang evidence, the Committee started their analysis by acknowledging that police officers have been accepted as expert witnesses in several different contexts across many common law jurisdictions[156].

The Committee considered that evidence of the associations of gangs fell into a similar category of evidence to that considered in *Hodges*:

> *"Evidence of the practices, mores and associations of gangs, whether general or particular, is in a similar category. It has been received in several jurisdictions and there can in principle be no objection to it being given by a police officer, providing that the ordinary threshold*

---

[155] [2016] UKPC 40

[156] Ibid, see para 57

> *requirements for expertise are established, and providing that the ordinary rules as to the giving of expert evidence are observed."*[157]

The Committee held that these two provisos are of particular importance. First, on whether expertise is established, the officer must:

> *"...have made a sufficient study, whether by formal training or through practical experience, to assemble what can properly be regarded as a balanced body of specialised knowledge which would not be available to the tribunal of fact...Care must be taken that simple, and not necessarily balanced, anecdotal experience is not permitted to assume the robe of expertise."*[158]

Secondly, on observing the ordinary rules of expert evidence, the Committee held that if a police officer is an expert, then he comes under the same duties to the court as any other expert.[159] The Committee went on to note that achieving compliance with these standards may be difficult for a police officer, as they are in effect combining the duties of an active investigator and independent expert.

Having considered that the evidence given by the police officer in each trial was sufficiently grounded in expertise, the Committee went on to consider at the duties of a police officer in presenting the evidence. These duties can now be located at part 19 of the Criminal Procedure Rules.

A number of cases followed *Myers* in which the principles surrounding the admissibility of expert evidence and duties on expert witnesses were considered. In *R v Khan*[160] the Court of Appeal considered whether a police officer, Detective Constable Reader, should have been treated as an expert witness. DC Reader was called at trial by the prosecution to give expert evidence about a gang called the Harlem Spartans. The

---

157 Idem

158 Ibid at [58]

159 Ibid at [59]

160 [2018] EWCA Crim 2893

prosecution relied on DC Reader's evidence to show that the Harlem Spartans were a pro-violence, anti-police gang which promoted the use of weapons and violence. In giving the judgment of the Court, Lord Justice Holroyde held:

> *"As to first of the rulings, DC Reader's evidence was that he had served in the police force for many years and had been extensively involved in the investigation of gang-related activity. The judge in our view was entitled to conclude that the officer had acquired sufficient expertise for it to be permissible for him to give opinion evidence as to whether the Harlem Spartans were exclusively a group of rap musicians or were rather, or in addition, a violent gang..."*[161]

Further, the Court held that the trial judge had been correct to reject the defence submission that the admission of the expert evidence of DC Reader would place the defence in an unfair position because the evidence would be impossible to challenge:

> *"...She pointed out that DC Reader could be cross-examined to suggest a different interpretation of what was seen or said and that the defendants would be able to give or to call evidence about the Harlem Spartans if they chose to do so. In our judgment, no successful criticism could be made of her decision. In the circumstances of this case, it was a decision which was not only open to her but in our view was plainly correct."*[162]

In *R v Shaveek Dixon-Kenton*[163] the Court of Appeal noted:

> *"Expert evidence about the existence of gangs, their ways of operating, their language and culture is increasingly adduced in the courts. Police officers in a number of cities have developed expertise in the gang*

---

[161] Ibid at para 20

[162] Ibid at para 22

[163] [2021] EWCA Crim 673

culture in the areas in which the police officers operate. That such evidence can be admissible is well recognised."[164]

In *Dixon-Kenton* the prosecution had served statements from a police officer (PC Barr) who had expertise in South London gangs. The prosecution sought to rely on the evidence to show that the defendant was part of a gang and had killed the victim, who was part of a rival gang, as part of a long running gang feud. The prosecution contended that PC Barr's evidence was admissible under section 98 of the Act, as it was evidence providing motive. Alternatively, it was admissible bad character evidence under section 101(1)(c) of the Act, as it provided important context to the actions of the defendant and, under section 101(1)(d) as it rebutted the defence of self-defence and loss of control and therefore went to an important issue in the case. PC Barr made a total of nine witness statements setting out the details of the rival gangs and a feud which had been running for ten years.

In relation to the officer's expertise the Court held that:

"PC Barr's expertise in respect of South London gangs, drill video lyrics, gang language etc was challenged on the application before the judge but not before us. It could not seriously be disputed that he was a recognised expert on London gangs. He had given evidence in over a dozen trials over the previous 3 years."[165]

The Court however acknowledged that disagreements between the parties may arise when an expert moves from the general to the particular:

"It does not follow from PC Barr's undoubted expertise in Lambeth gangs that he was entitled to assert, without more, that X or Y was a member of a particular (or any) gang. That opinion would have to be based on admissible evidence which could be tested in the usual way and which also satisfied the requirements of the CJA."

---

[164] Ibid at para 30

[165] Ibid at para 31

In *R v Heslop, Hassan and Constable*[166] the experience which qualified a police officer to give expert evidence on gangs was set out in the following agreed fact:

> *"8A. PS Paul Jones is a police officer who between 2014 and 2018 was in charge of investigating gang-related crime in the Borough of Harrow. PS Jones is experienced with gangs, how they operate and gang-related activity. In his opinion, for someone to deal drugs within the 'territory' of a gang, they would have to be dealing on behalf of the gang that controls that area."*

At the close of their case, the prosecution sought to rely on the evidence of PS Jones as it was argued he had direct dealings with most of the defendants and had extensive knowledge and experience of the gangs in Harrow. Further, it was argued that his evidence would assist the jury with the other evidence they had heard, including drill lyrics written by the defendants.

The defence at trial, relying on the test in *Myers*, argued that PS Jones should not be treated as an expert witness as, it was argued, he did not appear to be sufficiently trained in gangs and that any interactions he had had with the defendants would make him biased against them. On appeal the Court of Appeal recited the trial judge's reasons for allowing PS Jones to testify as to the existence of gangs before affirming the decision to admit the expert evidence:

> *"The judge noted that Police Sergeant Jones was in a position to testify about the existence of the gangs and to assist with their territories and rivalries. In the circumstances, he could act as an expert witness, applying the approach set out in Myers. Police Sergeant Jones had sufficient experience to act as an expert and was uniquely placed to assist the jury as to the circumstances in which the gangs conducted themselves in the relevant area. He was acquainted with these defendants, their culture and the nature of their feuds, and he would be warned to give the court a fair, independent and balanced account.*

[166] [2022] EWCA Crim 897

> *The judge observed that Police Sergeant Jones had known Constable from late 2016. He was acquainted with his street name, " Prime ", and was aware that he was a member of SCG. Constable regularly dealt in cannabis. He had £23,000 in his possession on arrest but was simultaneously homeless. He had no other obvious means of earning money. The judge determined that Mr Jones was entitled, furthermore, to give his opinion as to the likelihood that someone regularly dealing in cannabis in a particular area would have to be a member of the gang controlling the area.*[167]"

Finally, the Court clarified that *Myers* did not impose a precondition of a 'trigger event' for the introduction of gang related evidence:

> *"The judgment of Lord Hughes has been misunderstood in this regard. For the appellants Myers and Cox , it happened to be the position that an important strand in the 'rope of evidence' relied on by the prosecution was that there had been a trigger event which would have created a grievance within the opposing gang. As Lord Hughes observed, 'If that is a necessary part of the Crown case, it is for the Crown to prove the trigger event# (see [49]). The Privy Council did not, however, go further by imposing an obligation on the prosecution in every gang case to establish a relevant trigger event as a precondition for the admission of gang-related evidence*[168]"

Drill Music

Often part of the evidence which police officers are considering in gang related cases is 'drill music'. Drill is a breakaway genre from hip-hop and rap, originating from Chicago in 2012 before becoming popular in the UK, particularly in South London.

An early case in this area is *R v O.*[169] The appellant appealed against his conviction for possession of a firearm with intent to endanger life. At the

---

[167] Ibid at para 25

[168] Ibid at para 44

[169] [2010] EWCA Crim 2985

trial a YouTube video in which the appellant was rapping with others about gangs and firearms was admitted as evidence. Further, WPC Haynes, a local police officer, gave evidence relating to the YouTube video, including of her understanding of the purpose of the gang making the video, and of certain phrases used in the lyrics. She did not put herself forward as an expert and denied being one herself.

The appellant appealed on two grounds; the first, that the YouTube video should not have been admitted at all, and the second, that WPC Haynes' comments on the lyrics were improperly admitted as the opinion evidence of a non-expert. On the first ground the Court held that the video was properly admitted under gateway (d).

In relation to the second ground, the Court held:

> *"We turn therefore to the second ground of appeal which was that WPC Haynes' comments on the lyrics were improperly admitted as the opinion evidence of a non-expert. We consider that, as far as it goes, this ground is correct. It is perfectly true that WPC Haynes was put forward by the prosecution as someone with local insight and experience. We consider that much of the evidence that she gave about the situation of gangs in the locality and so forth was factual evidence, it might have been challenged evidence, but it was factual evidence, which was entirely admissible as coming from a police officer with local experience. It may even have been, if the ground had been properly laid, that that local experience would have been sufficient for her to have given evidence as a local expert. The word "expert" is slightly strange in these circumstances because it is, of course, very far removed from medical expertise or scientific or commercial expertise, but nevertheless there is no reason why a local person may not have expertise in a local dialect, and, as we have said, if the ground had been properly laid, it may well be that WPC Haynes was capable of being regarded as an expert in that limited sense about the language and patois of south London. However, the ground was not laid, and it was accepted from the beginning and accepted by her in evidence that she was not an expert. In those circumstances there was no basis for her to give*

> *opinion evidence, that is to say evidence that was not factual, evidence which may have lain outside the experience of a normal juryman.*
>
> *28. Nevertheless, even if some of her observations trespassed upon this ground of inadmissibility, the fact remains that much of the language of the lyrics was common ground. It was, as we have said, common ground that the lyrics as a whole were lyrics about guns and gun culture, as indeed other commercial lyrics have been, and that, as we have also said, the real issue between Crown and defence was whether this was art or life. That was an issue which we consider was plainly in the hands of the jury and the judge made very little of the detail of WPC Haynes' evidence. Indeed the relevant part of his summing-up dealing which the material that is objected to covers less than a well spaced and well margined page of the transcript.*
>
> *29. In the light of the very strong evidence of possession against the appellant and much other evidence besides of his participation in an allegiance to gang and gang culture in south London, we consider that the extent to which WPC Haynes' evidence may here and there, in dealing with particular words or phrases of the lyrics of the song, have trespassed beyond the general admissibility of her evidence would not, by any means, have affected the safety of this conviction. Therefore, although in principle we have accepted to some extent the basis of Mrs Smullen's second ground, we consider that these convictions remain safe. We therefore dismiss this appeal.*[170]"

The Court of Appeal clearly considered rap music capable of being a subject of expert evidence, but in cases where the language of the lyrics was clear to both parties and therefore formed common ground, it did not require expert interpretation – it was matter of fact rather than opinion. The Court left open the possibility of a police officer providing an expert interpretation of lyrics, if they set out how they were qualified to do so.

---

[170] Ibid at para 27-29

It is not just the lyrics of drill music which can support a prosecution case involving gang affiliation. In *Lewis*[171] , the police officers called as experts claimed that gangs "posted videos on the internet so as to announce the individuals' membership of the gang". A certain hand gesture made on the videos was said to be an indication of membership[172].

In *R v Awoyemi*[173] a YouTube video and notes of handwritten lyrics were admissible to "the extent to which the individuals concerned had signed up to gang and gun culture" and therefore of their propensity to commit offences which "bore all the hallmarks of gang related violence."[174]

R v Soloman[175] concerned an appellant who was convicted of possessing a firearm with intent to endanger life. The Court of Appeal considered two grounds of appeal. The second ground concerned the admissibility of a note found on one of the appellant's mobile telephones, which it was agreed had been created two days before the incident. The note appeared to be lyrics of a rap song of which the title line was "sold guns to str8 killers". This title line was admitted in evidence.

On the weight which should be attached to lyrics, the Court held:

> *"Turning to the second ground and the evidence of the rap lyric title, in our view that evidence was relevant for the reason given by the judge at the time he gave his decision to admit it that it was reasonably capable of being regarded as showing what was on the appellant's mind at the relevant time and as referring to the activity in which he was allegedly engaged, namely selling guns to street killers or potential killers. That said, the lyric seems to us of little weight in the context of this case, for the obvious reason that it appears to have been just that – a lyric – and that the lyrics of songs that people choose to record on their*

---

[171] [2014] EWCA Crim 48

[172] Ibid at para 44

[173] [2016] EWCA Crim 668

[174] Ibid at para 32-33

[175] [2019] EWCA Crim 1356

phones will often or perhaps typically have no connection to the factual reality of their own lives. That was a point which in our view, obvious as it might be, was one that it was necessary and appropriate for the judge to remind the jury of, either in his written directions or in his summing-up.[176]"

R v Rashid[177] involved allegations surrounding the possession of a firearm. The prosecution case was that Rashid and Tshoma were senior members of an East London gang called The Beckton Boys or ACG ('Anyone Can Go'). The trial judge, amongst other evidential issues, had to rule on the admissibility of the evidence of PC Saban as an expert in gangs, and his interpretation of lyrics in music videos.

The court considered the expert evidence given by a police officer on the music videos:

"First there is a complaint about the insubstantial nature of the evidence (participation in music videos and knowledge gleaned from social media as well as from unrevealed sources). In relation to evidence of this sort, the authorities are clear that a police officer may present expert evidence "of the practices, mores and association of gangs" see the Privy Council decision in Myers v Queen [2015] UKSC 40, [2016] AC 314 at paragraphs 57-61. Police officers are entitled to draw upon the body of expertise in this field, including the use of unidentified sources (see also Lewis at paragraphs 94 to 95).

49. In any event, PC Saban's opinion evidence that Tshoma was a gang member was to a large extent based on Tshoma's participation on two music videos, in one of which he could be seen with Issac Donkah and Rashid, and in one of which he could be seen brandishing a firearm, identifiable notwithstanding pixilation. As stated in Elliott [2010] EWCA Crim 2378 at paragraph 31:

[176] Ibid at para 12

[177] [2019] EWCA Crim 2018

> *Violent gangs, which provide no social amenity and exist for criminal purposes, are unlikely to issue membership cards, and so proof of membership will almost inevitably involve the prosecution putting forward evidence of a number of circumstances from which gang membership could be inferred.*
>
> *50. Proof of gang membership could be inferred from the particular videos in which he appeared and gang membership was celebrated. The prosecution made it clear that Tshoma was not seen or referenced in other gang videos featuring the other appellants and so there was no need for a specific direction to that effect.*[178]"

Cleary the Court of Appeal in *Rashid* considered the interpretation of drill music videos to be within the expertise of the police officer investigating the case, and that the appellant's designation as a gang member could be based on those videos to a "large extent."

[178] Ibid at para 48-50

CHAPTER TWELVE

AN INTRODUCTION TO FORENSIC SCIENCE

Forensic science is the application of science to a criminal investigation and court proceedings. Forensic science can play a significant role in a criminal investigation, from the initial report of the crime and the investigation at the scene, through the analysis and interpretation of the evidence collected and its role in guiding the criminal evidence, to its presentation in court.

Forensic science covers a broad range of disciplines: DNA, drugs, toxicology, firearms and ballistics, fire investigation, footwear comparison, fingerprint comparison, tool marks, trace evidence (glass, hair, paint, gunshot residue), questioned documents (handwriting etc), and digital forensics (recovery, analysis and interpretation of data from mobile phones).

Crime scene investigators (CSIs), also referred to as scene of crime officers (SOCOs) or forensic scene investigators (FSIs) undertake examination and interpretation of crime scenes to identify and recover relevant forensic evidence, which can prove or disprove if a crime has occurred. CSIs will search for DNA-rich material, fingerprints, footprints, and any other evidence (including on digital media), which will be submitted to a laboratory for examination and analysis.

Submissions include exhibits recovered by police investigators, for example, from suspects. Various examinations and tests will be carried out, with the results analysed and interpreted. The analysis and interpretation of the forensic evidence feeds into the evidential position of the overall case. The investigating officer will then decide how to proceed with the case.

Should the case lead to charge, further forensic evidence may be requested by either the prosecution or defence pre-trial to build a case to present before the court. Those conducting the examination or interpretation (or both), may be called to present evidence in person.

The following chapters considers a number of forms of forensic science as well as how statistics can be used to assess the value of the forensic evidence.

CHAPTER THIRTEEN

FINGERPRINT ANALYSIS

In 1892 Sir Francis Galton published his text *Finger Prints* on the use of fingerprints in solving crime. The text provided a compilation of research on fingerprints, highlighting how the unique nature of an individual's fingerprints could be used to assist identify an individual of interest in respect of a criminal act. Approximately 130 years later those theories and ideas are still prevalent with the identification and analysis of fingerprints found at crime scenes continuing to be a vital tool in the investigation of criminal allegations.

What is a fingerprint?

Approximately 95% of skin that covers the entire body is relatively smooth. Certain areas, for example fingers and palms of the hand and toes and soles of the feet, have friction ridges. These friction ridges help us hold onto objects. Within those friction ridges are pore openings with an associated sweat gland. Fingerprint deposits are produced from the secretions from those glands. Whilst the majority of the sweat deposited is moisture, there are trace amounts of other chemicals found in sweat. It is the deposition of those components that allow for the pattern of a fingerprint left on a surface that has been touched to be recovered and analysed.

No case has been found where an individual's finger or palm print has naturally changed over their lifetime. Equally everyone has a unique pattern on their fingers and palms. Consequently, fingerprint and palm prints have been found to be very useful in the investigation of crime.

How can fingerprints be recovered?

To utilise this means of identification the first step will be to recover prints from the scene of the alleged crime. The crime scene investigator will search for prints around key areas of the alleged crime – around the point of entry in an alleged burglary, or on items moved or left at the scene of a crime which may provide viable sources. Fingerprints will often be recovered in three sets of circumstances: those that are visible, those that are invisible to the naked eye, those that are formed in or on a suitably soft material (an impressed mark).

A visible fingerprint, when identified can be recorded using photography – the print is located, and a photograph taken to record the pattern of prints recorded. A visible print may be left when the fingers/palm have come into contact with a substance such as paint, ink or blood, which is then left on another surface following direct touch.

Fingerprints that are invisible to the naked eye are known as latent prints. They are made up of secretions from the sweat pores, which are left on the item touched when the moisture in sweat evaporates. The visualisation of those fingerprints invisible to the naked eye can be dealt with through powder dusting, chemical enhancement, or illumination methods.

Impressed marks are three dimensional marks formed when an item that is suitably soft is touched leaving the fingerprint impressed onto the material. Where an impressed mark is located the print can be photographed and sent for analysis.

The visualisation of latent prints is commonly approached in three ways – powder dusting, chemical enhancement, or illumination methods. Powder dusting is the application of powder with a handheld brush to the area being considered, with the powder particles sticking to the sweat components left at the scene. Chemical enhancement uses different chemicals (depending on the surface which is being considered) to develop and enhance the mark. The chemicals target specific components in the fingerprint composition and attach themselves to it to make the mark visible, at which point it can be photographed for analysis. Illumination methods expose the fingerprint to UV or laser lights. Certain substances in sweat fluoresce when exposed to these types of lights.

The examination of fingerprints

Upon receipt of the fingerprint lifts or photographs from the crime scene the marks will be checked against any elimination samples, including the police elimination database. Just as other forms of forensic evidence require the elimination of those that had legitimate reason to touch an item (whether purposely or inadvertently), so does fingerprint evidence.

The print will then be scanned onto the national fingerprint database, known as IDENT1. The IDENT1 system searches the database to present a list of people with marks that bear close similarity to the mark left at the crime scene. The population of the IDENT1 database will have come from people who have been arrested and charged, reported, or summoned for a recordable offence, and have had their fingerprints taken.

Fingerprint patterns can be divided into three groups – arches, loops, and whorls – describing the shape of the ridges. Those patterns can then be subdivided further. These patterns and sub patterns make up the characteristics of the fingerprint (known as the 'Galton characteristics'). There are seven basic ridge characteristics: ridge ending, bifurcation, lake, independent ridge, dot or island, spur, and crossover.

In undertaking a search and comparison with the sample obtained from the crime scene the first step will be for the sample obtained to be assessed for quality. The mark will be reviewed for whether any ridge detail can be observed, and whether it is sufficient for comparison purposes. The mark will then be compared against the suspects (having been taken in custody) or run through IDENT1. The comparison process involves the expert considering the ridge marks on the two prints being compared.

The examination process in relation to crime scene marks consists of stages of analysis, comparison, evaluation, and verification (ACE-V). The expert will assess the impression to determine whether it is suitable for comparison, noting, for example, the material upon which the impression has been deposited, any enhancement process undertake, and the clarity of the print. The examiner will then compare the samples provided. The expert will consider what class of characteristic the print falls within (arches, loops, or whorls), before considering the individual minutiae characteristics (ridge endings, etc) and considering the distribution of the pores in the print. The comparison can either be manual (through the use of hard copy images) or computer based (using onscreen images). It is the evaluation of the class and individual characteristics that allow the fingerprint examiner to offer an opinion on whether a positive identification can be made. The process is not a statistical evaluation, but instead based on the expert's opinion formed against their own competence, experience, and skill. When conducting a comparison, it is important that the examiner records and keeps records of how that decision has been made.[179] Finally verification will take place. This is the independent assessment of the prints by an independent examiner.

For an identification to be confirmed at least 16 points of agreement and no more than 0 points of disagreement must be matched. Evidently if there is a point of disagreement between the lifted sample and the suspect's fingerprints the individual can be excluded as the person who left the mark. If sufficient points of similarity are found the examiner may conclude the mark found at the crime scene can be identified to the person. If it is considered that there are levels of significant disagreement between the impressions, the examiner will consider the individual is excluded as a potential donor of the unknown print. If the quality of the available prints is such that the impression if lacking in quality the examiner will record the impression as insufficient. Where the quality provides for some levels of agreement, but not to such a level as to be a conclusive match, the examiner may mark the outcome as inconclusive. Where there is any difference in opinion between examiners this should be noted in the case file and ultimately disclosed in accordance with the Criminal Procedure and Investigations Act 1996.[180]

---

[179] In accordance with ISO/IEC 17025

[180] Forensic Science Regulator Codes – Fingerprint Comparison FSR-C-128 at para 6.4.4

Whilst the shape of the ridge marks will be the primary source of consideration for identification purposes other characteristics of a fingerprint, such as the general direction of the ridges, the overall pattern type, the positioning of pores and features such as scars can be used as part of the identification process.

Obtaining fingerprints from suspected individuals

Section 61 of the Police and Criminal Evidence Act 1984 allows the police to take fingerprints from detained persons. Whilst consent is generally required from the person whose fingerprints are to be taken at the police station, consent is not required if the individual is detained as a result of the individual's arrest for a recordable offence and they have not had their full set of fingerprints taken during the course of the investigation for that offence, or the set was of insufficient quality.

Where an individual is released from being detained at the police station, prints may subsequently be taken without consent if, during the initial period of detention fingerprints were not taken.

Further a constable may take a person's fingerprints without consent if the constable suspects the person is committing or attempting to commit, or has committed or attempted to commit an offence and the identity of that person is unknown and cannot be readily ascertained by the constable, or there exists reasonable grounds for doubting the name given by the person as being their real name.

The use of fingerprints in the criminal justice system

Finding a fingerprint on an item can be used to show that the person matched with the print has, at some point, come into direct contact with the item where the prints are located. Unlike DNA that can be transferred through secondary or tertiary transfer, fingerprints can only be left directly by the person whose print it is.

However, fingerprints cannot be aged. It is not possible to say when, or in what circumstances the item has been touched. Consequently, in the case of prints left on items that can readily be moved from one place to another, the print cannot say when the item or the items examined was left at the scene of the alleged crime. Investigators may make enquiries of when surfaces/items were last cleaned/wiped down and identified to be at the scene to narrow time frames.

Risk of Cognitive Bias

The assessment and interpretation of fingerprints is subjective in nature. It is based on an individual's skill, experience, and judgement. Consequently, it has the potential for different examiners to arrive at different conclusions. The starting point for the examination may differ between examiners, equally the visibility of particular features may vary.

But the subjective interpretative nature of fingerprint identification also increases the possibility of cognitive bias. Cognitive bias is an error in thinking affecting an individual's decision making. When improperly managed, cognitive bias could impact on the reliability of the examination outcome. The Forensic Science Regulator Codes of Practice and Conduct acknowledges the potential risk of cognitive bias in fingerprint comparison. [181] It requires organisations put in place safeguards to minimise the risk of cognitive bias, for example blind verification.

Cognitive bias can be categorised as contextual, confirmation and cultural. Contextual bias occurs because of the contextual information that an expert is exposed to during their instruction. This will include the nature and details of the crime, any previous criminal activity of the suspect, the location of the crime and any media interest in the allegation. Prior knowledge of this contextual information can influence the decision-making process of a fingerprint examiner. Confirmation bias can occur during examination requests received from police officers or

---

[181] Forensic Science Regulator Codes of Conduct and Practice Fingerprint Comparison FSR-C-128 at para 6.1.2 available at https://assets.publishing.service.gov.uk/government/uploads/system/uploads/attachment_data/file/638254/128_FSR_fingerprint_appendix__Issue2.pdf

prosecution services, as the instruction will often be on the basis that the identification will help 'solve the crime' or 'secure a conviction'. Examiners may be influenced by confirmation bias when, having found a number of features that suggest a match, they then begin to reason backwards by finding features in the unknown impression that are suggested by those in the known print rather than being visible without reference to the known source material. Cultural bias may include over confidence if opinions are not challenged but merely accepted, a lack of interaction with peers resulting in limited exposure to alternative methods of working, and a lack of acceptance of the potential for errors.

This risk of cognitive bias was highlighted in a 2005 research project by Dror and others.[182] Whilst using a relatively small sample size, the study noted that in cases where fingerprints comparison was ambiguous (rather than clear non-matching prints) examiners were more likely to find a match when they had been provided with information such as photographs from crime scenes and background stories to the incident they were considering. The study concluded that such contextual information actively biases the way gaps are filed in the examiners mind when drawing conclusions. A further study in 2006 by the same authors provided examiners with prints they had previously concluded were a match but, additionally provided contextual information to suggest they were in fact not a match. With the new context most of the fingerprint experts made a different judgement to that they had previously made when the contextual information had not been provided.

[182] Dror e al. (2005) "When Emotions get the better of us: The effect of contextual top-down processing on matching fingerprints", Applied Cognitive Psychology, Wiley, followed up by Dror, et al. (2006) 'Contextual Information Renders Experts Vulnerable to Making Erroneous Identifications', Forensic Science International, 156

The Forensic Science Regulator Code of Conduct for Fingerprint Comparison requires those involved in fingerprint examination to put in place methods to mitigate against this risk of cognitive bias[183]. One possible way of mitigating against cognitive bias will be to introduce blind verification. The starting point for this will be to limit the amount of information the examiner has, whilst providing them with enough to be able to conduct the exercise. Removing contextual information that adds no tangible value to the examination process removes the potential for contextual bias. A blind verification process can assist by limiting from within the process knowledge of how the identification request has come to be at the hands of the examiner.

The effect of cognitive bias was seen in the highly publicised cases of Shirley McKie and Brandon Mayfield.

The case of Shirley McKie involved the murder of Marion Ross in Kilmarnock in 1997. McKie was a detective assigned to help in the case. Fingerprints were found at the crime scene, including a print on a bathroom doorframe. A match came back to McKie, who denied ever being inside the crime scene. Matches also came back to a potential suspect, David Asbury. During the trial of Asbury (who was convicted of Ross' murder) McKie denied leaving the prints at the bathroom doorframe. Following Asbury's conviction McKie was arrested and charged with perjury for denying that she was at the crime scene. Following a trial McKie was unanimously found not guilty after several fingerprint experts independently gave an opinion that the supposed match was incorrect. Given the errors in McKie's fingerprints, Asbury successfully challenged his conviction after judges accepted that the fingerprint evidence was unreliable. A subsequent public inquiry found McKie was the victim of human error in the conclusions drawn during

[183] Forensic Science Regulator Cognitive Bias Effects Relevant to Forensic Science Examinations FSR-G-217 at 8.5

the fingerprint analysis, and there was nothing sinister at work in her case.[184]

During the course of the investigation into the Madrid bombings in March 2004 a blue plastic bag containing detonators was found near the scene of the bombings. A latent print was taken from the bag, with the FBI provided with a digital copy. An American lawyer who had converted to Islam was identified by the FBI as a match to the fingerprint – Brandon Mayfield. Mr Mayfield was arrested and detained for two weeks whilst investigations took place. Spanish authorities disputed the FBI's analysis. Upon viewing the original image, it became clear an error had been made and Mayfield was released. A subsequent US Department of Justice report[185] into the handling of the case concluded that, whilst Mayfield's fingerprint did have an unusual similarity with the latent print, having located as many as 10 points of similarity the examiners undertaking the comparison began to 'find' additional features that were not really there (i.e. a form of cognitive bias through backward reasoning). Further undue weight was given by the examiners to extremely tiny details and the examiners were overconfident in their explanations for differences in appearance between the latent print and that of Mayfield. The inquiry concluded that the examiners were not aware of Mayfield's religion and so this did not play a part in their erroneous conclusions. The Mayfield case provides a good example of how cognitive bias can unduly influence examiners to reach the wrong conclusion despite their own confidence in their conclusions.

184 https://cdn.southampton.ac.uk/assets/imported/transforms/content-block/UsefulDownloads_Download/CAA0EC21E7594E37BDE4BE125961830B/2011-12-13%20Chairmans%20address.pdf

185 Available at https://oig.justice.gov/special/s0601/final.pdf

CHAPTER FOURTEEN

FIREARMS

A case involving firearms can often involve a multitude of expert witnesses. DNA may be present on areas of the firearm. Fingerprints may be on the handle or trigger. Visual expertise may be required in the identification of suspects from local CCTV. But importantly experts involved in the analysis of firearms can be used to identify the firearm, match weapons with used bullets and assist to provide a reconstruction of events.

The firearms expert will focus their analysis on ballistics (examining what happens to a bullet when inside the barrel of a firearm, during flight and when it reaches its target), gunshot residue (examining the hands or clothing of individuals believed to have come into contact with the fired weapon), and determining the make, model and serial number of a firearm. The key questions to be addressed will often be identification of the type of weapon used, establishing the distance between the victim and the weapon, determining the direction of impact, identifying the type of ammunition used, establishing the sequence of shots, whether discharge was accidental or intentional, and identifying any links between scenes where appropriate.

The National Ballistics Intelligence Service provides a national database of confidential information on firearms recovered in the UK, with associated ballistic information. It provides an intelligence tool for linking incidents, locations, and suspects to firearms.

Firearms

The basic premise of a firearm and how a projectile is fired is that the firearm converts chemical energy into kinetic energy in order to expel a projectile from the firearm. Following a round being loaded and locked into the breach of the firearm, as the trigger is pulled back the hammer mounted firing pin is forced to strike through a small hole in the breach hitting the primer. This creates a chemical burn, producing hot gases which ignite the propellant in the cartridge of the bullet. The expansion of gas propels the bullet down the barrel of the firearm.

Section 57(1) Firearms Act 1968 interprets 'firearm' as being a lethal barrelled weapon, a prohibited weapon, a relevant component part in relation to either a lethal barrelled or prohibited weapon, or an accessory to such a weapon designed or adapted to diminish the noise or flash caused by firing the weapon. A lethal barrelled weapon is a barrelled weapon from which a shot, bullet, or other missile with kinetic energy of more than one joule at the muzzle of the weapon can be discharged. A relevant component part is a barrel, chamber or cylinder, a frame, body or receiver, or a breech block bolt or other mechanism for containing the pressure of discharge at the rear of a chamber capable of being used as part of a lethal barrelled weapon or prohibited weapon. A prohibited weapon is one found in s5 of the Firearms Act 1968 and includes a wide range of weapons including CS sprays and tasers, as well as rocket launchers and mortars (but not those designed for pyrotechnic purposes).

An imitation weapon (as defined in s57 Firearms Act 1968) is defined as anything which has the appearance of being a firearm (other than those already identified as prohibited weapons) whether or not it is capable of discharging any shot, bullet or other missile.

Crime Scene Investigation

In any case involving a firearm there can be several separate crime scenes. This can include the location where a victim has sustained a firearms related injury, the location where a victim has been found, the location where the firearm was discharged, and any place where the firearm was located. Each location will need to be assessed for the potential of evidence that a firearms expert can assist in analysing and interpreting.

Where the recovery of evidence is difficult as the crime scene cannot be immediately secured and preserved, officers will be encouraged to utilise body worn cameras to film the scene, including the locations of key features (damage, firearms, ballistics, etc).

Where a firearm is located at the scene of the crime the priority will be to make it safe. Photographs will often be taken of the scene, including showing items in the location that they have been found. Bullet holes, blood patterns and cartridge cases will all be in the mind of the examiner. The firearm left at the scene will be left in situ until made safe by a firearms officer. Only when made safe will the item be then considered by the Crime Scene Investigator, including photographing the item. The firearm will be secured in a box, noting the made safe certificate completed by the firearms officer. If wet, the firearm will not be packaged in plastic as rust will develop and can change the marks left in any test firings. When submitted for testing, the firearm and ammunition will be kept separate. It will also be kept separate from any exhibits taken from the suspect or the victim.

The condition of the firearm will be considered by the expert, as well as recovering trace evidence. Consideration should be given to the potential presence of DNA and fingerprints on the firearm, although this process should only be completed when safe and under the supervision of the firearms expert to avoid any unintentional discharge. The firearm will be packaged for transportation to the laboratory for further analysis.

The analysis of the firearm will involve noting its serial number, printed into the firearm. The process of stamping the number onto the firearm also impresses the digits below the surface of the metal. Consequently, scratching off the serial number will not remove the indentation underneath the serial number. That number can be identified using a process of microscopy, oblique lighting, or chemical visualisation. The analysis of the firearm includes an assessment of its condition. This will include whether it has any safety catches and its position, whether a round is in the breech, and whether that round is live or spent.

When an injury has been caused by a gunshot the resultant blood pattern will appear as a mist like dispersion of blood. Features of the wounds can assist in determining the distance from which the individual was shot.

Contact wounds will be located at the location where the firearm came into contact with the skin of the person. The burning mixture of the primer and propellant gases causes a burn mark around the point of contact. Where contact was with clothing, the mark is left on the clothing rather than the skin. Where the shot has been taken up to 1m away a circular entrance would be created, with a shading around the wound caused by the propellant and primer residues. The shape of the shading can assist establish the angle at which the weapon was fired. Where the distance is over 1m there will be no shading. Where the firearm has been fired at great distance, the required energy to propel the ballistic is much greater, causing more severe internal injuries.

Further the resultant propellant can be tested for DNA and fingerprint evidence. Whilst the heat generated in the barrel may be detrimental to the quality of the evidence, as technology improves the potential for quality evidence cannot be discounted.

Ballistics

Different types of firearms will use different projectiles, each with distinctive characteristics. One of the primary methods of categorising bullets is through their calibre. This is the diameter of the bullet. The calibre of the bullet however does not necessarily prove the calibre of the weapon as on occasion a bullet too large or too small may be used. Ammunition is composed of a cartridge case or jacket, a primer, a propellant, and a bullet. All commercially available ammunition is stamped with a mark (known as the cartridge headstamp) that can be found on the base of the cartridge and used to identify the manufacturer, calibre, and date of production.

Bullets do not follow a straight line. They are subject to drag, air resistance and gravity causing them to follow a downward arc rather than a straight line. The presence of grooves within the barrel can cause a bullet to spin on its axis during flight which can change its path. Whilst the initial speed of the bullet is dependent on the initial force applied to it, that will change when air residence and drag reduce its energy.

What happens to a bullet when it hits its intended target depends on the energy that remains on impact. Low velocity weapons cause damage by the penetration of the bullet with the intended target. High velocity weapons create both a point of penetration and a cavity as a result of the oscillating shock waves after the bullet has passed through.

Ballistic examination will consider the ballistic over three stages. Firstly, an internal ballistic examination will consider the mechanics of what happens inside a firearm from the point that the firing pin hits the primer to the moment the ballistic exits the firearm. The focus of the examination will consider the scrapes made to the ballistic on the internal ridges of the muzzle as it is fired. External ballistics is concerned with the behaviour of the ballistic in flight. The trajectory, range and momentum of a bullet can be established to assist in reconstructing events. Terminal ballistics consider the behaviour of the projectile as it hits its target. This breaks down to the ability of the ballistic to penetrate various materials, and the ability of the ballistic to damage living tissue. This can assist establish what type of weapon was used and the distance between the weapon and where it struck.

Rifling and Identification

During the manufacture of the firearms barrel, a series of lands and grooves are produced along the inside of the barrel, known as rifling. A land is a raised portion of indentations, whereas the grooves are the lower portions between these lands. The internal rifling in the barrel is a design feature which provides the bullet with a degree of spin when fired. That increases the stability and accuracy of the trajectory when it is fired. The rifling will leave microscopic scratches on the bullet when it is fired (known as 'striations').

This process is based on the principle that a relatively soft bullet will pass down a harder steel barrel, at which point the helical set of grooves and lands in the bore will engrave the surface of the bullet. The forensic expert will consider the significance of the transferred marks on the basis of their class, sub class and individual marks. Class marks are common to a type of firearm, for example the number of rifling grooves and lands that a particular model of firearm has. Sub class marks are unintentional manufacturing marks transferred to a particular firearm during the manufacturing process. Individual marks are the general 'wear and tear' marks caused during the use of the firearm.

When the firearm is test fired, the scratches left on the test bullet will be compared against those left at the scene to consider whether the marks on the test bullet match those on the bullets found at the crime scene. That process allows the bullets to be matched to the firearm. The number of marks, and the widths between them, plus the direction and degree of twist on a fired bullet differs between makes and models of firearms, which can then be checked against a database of previously known weapons to establish a match.

The principal skill required by the expert is pattern recognition (much like fingerprint experts). The interpretation is subjective in nature, requiring a second examiner to verify the findings of the first examiners results. A five-point scale can be used to explain the findings (although a three point scale can also be used):

Conclusive identification – the class characteristics match and the individual characteristics are distinctive.

Strong identification – the class characteristics match, although the individual characteristics raised some doubts because of imperfections in the striations.

Inconclusive identifications – the class characteristics match, but no distinctive similarities or differences in the individual characteristics could be found.

Limited identification – the class characteristics match, but differences exist in the individual characteristics which could be explained by wear, corrosion, or deliberate alteration of the firearm. There is in this circumstance more disagreement than agreement. This tends to suggest the firearm was not used to fire the individual ballistic.

Exclusion – Even if the class characteristics match, the individual characteristics may show clear differences which cannot have occurred due to changes in the machine components.

Firearm Discharge Residue

When a firearm is discharged, the primer and propellant are expelled from any gaps in the weapon in a cloud of gas and fine particles. The cloud of material is referred to as firearm discharge residue ('FDR'). FDR contains particles of propellant and combustion materials produced by the hot gases acting on the bullet when it is fired. The FDR will be deposited on the person firing the weapon.

When a weapon is discharged gunshot residue deposited on nearby surfaces can be used to assess the distance at which the firearm was discharged. The more concentrated the residue pattern, the closer to the point of firing.

Gunshot residues can be collected using a swabbing, film lifts or adhesive tape. Once collected the residue will be analysed and compared both physically and chemically. The chemical composition of the residue can be assessed and provide a link between the crime scene, firearm and persons involved. However, the loss of particles of FDR can be rapid. Acts such as washing and general movement will reduce the amount of FDR deposited. Consequently, transfer of FDR material is a real risk. Firearms officers must be alive to the possibility of cross contamination between the handling of different weapons.

A suspect's clothing should be removed carefully, item by item, to ensure any debris falling off is caught, which can later be exhibited.

CHAPTER FIFTEEN

THE USE OF DNA IN CRIMINAL PROCEEDINGS

Like many people of my generation my awareness of DNA was first introduced as a tool that could be used to bring dinosaurs back to life. 27 years later I am still waiting for the reintroduction of Stegosaurus and Brachiosaurus back into society – clearly something has not quite worked out. Whilst DNA has not (yet) been used to develop dinosaur themed parks it does have many significant uses, particularly in the criminal justice system.

An overview of the science

Deoxyribonucleic acid (or 'DNA') is present in almost every cell in the human body. The DNA of relevance to forensic science used in the criminal justice system is found in the nucleus (the controlling mind) of a cell[186]. This is known as genomic DNA. It provides the complete genetic information of a person, containing a record of each person's individual features.

Whilst identified by Swiss biochemist Johan Friedrich Miescher in 1869, it was not until 1953 when James Watson and Francis Crick revealed the structure of DNA and provided an explanation how the genetic information is passed from generation to generation. In the mid 1980's research undertaken by Dr Alec Jefferies demonstrated that certain area of the DNA strand contained patterns, and that these patterns varied between individuals (except for identical twins/triplets). Dr Jefferies

[186] DNA can also be found in mitochondrial DNA which serve as cell 'power plants'

demonstrated how this technique could be used to identify individuals by comparing samples of DNA.

DNA presents itself in the form of a double helix. Unwinding the double helix structure leads to two long strands in a ladder-like structure. Each 'rung' of the DNA ladder contains two of the four chemical bases, held together by a hydrogen bond. The four chemical bases are adenine ('A), thymine ('T'), guanine ('G') and cytosine ('C'). The four bases pair up in a particular manner: adenine with thymine, and guanine with cytosine. It is the subsequent order up and down the ladder of those paired up bases that give DNA its unique profile and we as humans our unique profiles.

Within human DNA there are approximately 3 billion base pairs (an AT or CG combination) and approximately 20,000 – 25,000 genes[187] all containing genetic information. However over 98% of human DNA is non-coding and does not serve a purpose for forensics. This includes 'fossil genes' (those that may have had a use in the past, but no longer do), sequences that have no function, and sequences where we simply do not know their function.

Genomic DNA arranges itself into the form of chromosomes. All body cells, with the exception of 'sex cells' have 23 pairs of chromosomes – 46 in total (23 from the male, 23 from the female). Sex cells (sperm cells in men, egg cells in women) contain only 23 chromosomes. When an egg is fertilised by sperm the resultant fertilised egg (a zygote cell) contains the fused 46 chromosomes. All 75- 100 trillion cells in the human body originate from this single cell.

Whilst cells can be grouped into different tissue types performing different functions, including blood, saliva, bone or muscle, what is consistent (with the exception of sex cells and mutations) is the DNA profile in each. DNA remains consistent throughout human life.

---

[187] A gene is a DNA sequence providing an individual characteristic

Each pair of chromosomes is numbered 1–22. The final pair are the sex chromosomes, X and Y, which determine the sex of the individual. A male will have XX sex chromosomes, with a female having XY sex chromosomes.

When reviewing an expert report on DNA a number of key terms often recur:

- A chromosome: As addressed above, one of 23 pairs found in the nucleus of cells, from which DNA can be extracted

- A locus (sometimes referred to as a DNA marker): a place on the chromosome where a gene can be found. A particular gene will always be located on a particular place on the chromosome. The plural of locus, often referred to in experts' reports is loci.

- A gene: a specific sequence of DNA molecules.

- An allele: an individual will inherit two allele (one from the male, one from the female) which are located on a gene at the gene's locus on the chromosome. The DNA sequencing on a particular allele will produce an individual characteristic.

It is the analysis of the sequence of DNA that is of use to the criminal justice system.

An overview of the use of DNA in the Criminal Justice System

DNA has had a huge impact on the investigation of crime. DNA evidence looks at patterns in a suspect's DNA and compares it to a pattern in the DNA on, or at, the crime scene (whatever that may be).

The present system of analysis of DNA is known as 'DNA17'. Introduced in July 2014 it replaced the previous system of SGM Plus ('Second Generation Multiplex'). DNA17 harmonised the approach across Europe benefiting cross border exchange of information. DNA17 considers 16 STR loci, plus the sex locus. SGM plus was introduced in

1999 to replace the previous system of (perhaps unsurprisingly named) SGM. SGM plus considered 10 STR loci plus the sex chromosomes, whereas SGM considered 6. SGM was introduced in 1995 replacing a previous system that considered 4 STR loci. As the process has developed, and the number of loci used to compare increased, the level of accuracy has increased.

However, it is not without risk. Increases in technology have allowed for DNA profiles to be obtained from increasingly smaller samples – but as the sensitivity of techniques improves, so does the risks of transfer and contamination. It is paramount that samples are handled carefully to avoid contamination and cross transfer. Practitioners should have a clear awareness of the chain of custody of the samples in consideration of where the potential for contamination and cross transfer could have occurred.

Sources of DNA

There are many items that can be recovered from a crime scene that will potentially bear DNA. Millions of skin cells are shed from the body every day and these will inevitably be contained in other bodily secretions, such as blood, saliva, mucus and sweat.

Blood: It is the role of red blood cells to carry oxygen and other nutrients around the body. These cells do not contain DNA. For the purposes of DNA analysis it is white blood cells that are required. When a person bleeds the first line of defence of the body is to try and stop the bleeding. It does this by flushing white blood cells to the wound, and consequently out of the body. Damaged skin cells will be picked up with the white blood cells in the initial flow. Red blood cells (containing no DNA) will follow. Consequently a better sample of DNA will be obtained closer to the site where the wounding took place – conversely a sample of blood may not be usable for DNA analysis where it is further away from the site of wounding.

Semen: DNA material can be located in the head of spermatozoa. It is possible to identify a sample as semen through a search for seminal acid phosphatase or a protein specific antigen in the sample.

Saliva: Saliva can often be found on items such as bottle tops. The focus of the analysis will be on the skin cells from the inside of the mouth (buccal cells) that will have transferred to the item. Acidic and sugary drinks may degrade the sample from the bottle top, thereby affecting the quality of the sample obtained. The best surfaces for obtaining DNA are rigid/serrated areas where cells may be torn away from touch.

Sweat: Sweat does not contain cellular material in its pure form, but (as with saliva) may contain skin cells present within the sweat stain. An area of clothing, such as the armpit or close-fitting areas will tend to be the focus of the examination.

Mucus: If a used handkerchief/tissue is recovered mucus can provide a good source of DNA. The force utilised when sneezing or coughing can result in skin cells from the lining of the nose or mouth to be present. Where spit is located on a pavement, it can be swabbed and assessed for a sample.

Urine: Unlikely to contain cellular material having passed through the urethra.

Hair: The shaft of the hair simply contains dead cells and so will rarely be suitable for analysis, although mitochondrial DNA can be extracted from a hair sample without a root. In order to obtain sufficient cellular material for analysis, hair with a root is needed. Hair that has fallen out naturally (and therefore likely to be found in hats/scarfs etc) is dead hair and therefore does not have a root. Where hair with a root is located, this may be evidence of some force used to pull it out.

Faeces: Faeces contains bacteria which degrades DNA and consequently is not generally suitable for analysis.

Dandruff: Dead skill cells, and therefore not suitable for analysis.

The Evidential Process of obtaining DNA

Turning a sample of DNA obtained on a swab to something that can be used in the court process takes the sample through several stages. As the sensitivity of DNA profiling techniques increases, so does the risk of cross transfer and contamination. Consequently, first responders to a crime scene will need to be aware of the potential risks of contamination from the outset.

Procedures to assist in avoiding the risk of contamination and cross transfer may include the following:

- Appropriate personal protective equipment: to limit the potential for new DNA to be introduced at the crime scene, or during the procedure of analysis.

- Storage: Samples taken from the complainant and suspect should be stored away from each other to ensure no contact takes place.

- Cleaning and maintenance: To avoid the risk of cross contamination and transfer from work on other samples.

- Elimination databases: Both laboratory specific and police samples should be obtained to eliminate people who have legitimately come into contact with the sample.

The process of extracting DNA involves the following steps:

Obtaining a Sample – a sample is located at a crime scene or speculative swabs are taken from sites likely to hold samples of evidential value. The sample is subsequently passed to the laboratory for the extraction and analysis.

Extraction and Purification – The sample is checked for cells from which DNA can be extracted. The process of extraction and purification involves disrupting the cells obtained from the crime scene, removing of the non-nucleic components of the cells leaving the DNA, and concentration of the remaining nucleic acids. In order to isolate the DNA the sample will go through a series of solutions to remove the unnecessary parts. In order to separate the final nucleic acids a process of electrophoresis is undertaken, with a supporting medium to act as a molecular sieve enabling DNA fragments to be separated on the basis of their respective sizes.

Quantification – The DNA extracted from the cells is then quantified. The DNA sample will be measured in terms of the numbers of base pairs that have been obtained. The sample of DNA can then be measured by a process of spectrophotometry. Where the DNA concentration of a sample is low, an alternative process of quantification may be used: spectrofluorimetry.

Amplification – If sufficient DNA has been obtained, the DNA goes through a process known as a polymerase chain reaction. The process enables the designated loci to be duplicated many times over, allowing for detection and interpretation. The technique involves a process of repeatedly heating, cooling and stretching the sample. As the number of cycles of the process repeats the number of DNA fragments will exponentially increase in size.

Detection – DNA is transmitted through a laser causing the chemical labels on the DNA fragments to fluoresce, allowing them to be detected by a scanner and recorded by a computer. Genetic mapping and sequencing have shown regions between the non-coding regions of the DNA strand that differ between individuals (termed 'minisatellite DNA'). These regions are found at various sites throughout the genome. Each minisatellite contains a sequence of bases ('A', 'T', 'C' or 'G') which is repeated. This is used to identify individuals based on their DNA profile. The repeats of the base pairs represent a distinct allele carried on a chromosome. Where the repeat is short in the length of the number of base pairs (a short tandem repeat – 'STR') following the process of amplification the variation in length of the alleles is easier to distinguish than those repeats with a greater length of number of base pairs.

Interpretation – software is used to interpret the computer-generated data. The intensity of each light position is displayed as a peak on an electropherogram. The height of the peak gives an indication of the amount of DNA present in the sample – small peaks can be described as low levels of DNA, whereas high peaks result from a greater amount of DNA being present in the test sample. The peaks are compared, to establish whether the samples are from the same person, or not. Even in a largely automated technological process, human judgement continues to play its part. The skill and experience of a forensic scientist will be applied to validate results.

Interpreting the Electropherogram

The final stage of the process of extraction of DNA from the sample that has been obtained involves the production of charts showing a series of 'bars' of differing length and width, known as an electropherogram. The data produced is analysed by the scientists to determine the significance of the specific bars at particular locus and interpret the results through an act of comparison.

DNA profiling requires a comparative approach, involving the analysis of two or more profiles to establish whether the patterns match. DNA samples will have been obtained from at least two crime 'scenes': the place of the offence, and the suspected offender. The skill of the forensic scientist is the ability to determine whether the two can be brought together.

An analysis of the DNA profile obtained from the site examined can lead to the following potential results:

- Full profile – a DNA profile containing information on all alleles within a marker system. This would produce all 17 loci from the sample obtained.

- Partial profile – not all 17 loci are present from the sample obtained. This may be because of the quality of the sample. The sample can be affected by environmental factors, including exposure to sunlight, acids (in carbonated drinks) or other chemicals (including dyes used in denim).

- Mixed profile – this will be evident where a particular locus contains DNA from more than one individual. This will be evidenced from there being more than 2 peaks at each particular locus. Ordinarily one would expect two peaks, representing two alleles (one from the male, one from the female). Where there are more than two this is indicative of a mixed sample. A mixed profile may produce a major/minor component or an equivalent ratio. Sometimes one person's DNA is present in a greater amount than the other persons. This may result in clearly defined differences in the peak heights of the chart, so that it is easy to tell the stronger major profile from the weaker minor profile. In other samples the difference in peak heights may not be sufficiently different to be able to distinguish between one profile from another.

The DNA profile, as evidenced by the computer printout of peaks and troughs, has a baseline level of background noise. Background noise will show itself through an artificial peak on the graph. Different testing kits produce different levels of background noise. Consequently, some kits will be better than others when dealing with lower levels of DNA in a sample as they are less sensitive to background noise, and therefore the artificial peaks can be distinguished from genuine peaks more clearly[188]. The role of the expert will be to assess whether a peak represents a true allele or that is represents background noise.

If any of the two compared loci do not match, then the interpretation is conclusive – the DNA samples are not from the same person. The evidential use of the sample is therefore to establish that the individual

[188] See 'Sensitivity and baseline noise of three new generation forensic autosomal STR kits: Powerplex fusion, Verifiler Plus and Investigator 24plex QS' by Tay and others for further information on how background noise can vary between testing kits. Available at https://www.sciencedirect.com/science/article/pii/S2665910719300490

who provided the sample not found at the crime scene was not the individual who deposited the sample recovered from the crime scene.

However, where there is a match between the two profiles it then becomes necessary to consider whether the match obtained has simply occurred by chance (i.e., a false positive).

Establishing the evidential significance of a match

Whether a match between two unrelated individuals has been obtained as a result of chance will generally be expressed in the form of a probability. The strength of DNA evidence is reflected by the value of the probability of a match between DNA profiles from the crime sample and the accused that is random. Practitioners reading this book may well be familiar with the oft quoted '1 in a billion' statistic. Of course, the resultant probability is not 1 in a billion – it is far greater than that. The 1 in a billion figure is considered significant enough to make the point required from the analysis.

In order to calculate that probability, it is required to know the relative frequency of a particular allele occurring at a locus point within the general population. The population of a relevant ethnicity is taken into account. This allows us to establish the probability that a particular allele occurring at a particular locus from the general population.

The Forensic Science Regulator oversees the frequency databases for use with DNA profiles. All forensic profiles now use the same five allele frequency databases based on ethnicity (updated in 2014): white (2550 alleles), black African/Caribbean (770 alleles), South Asian (400 alleles), East and South East Asian (406 alleles), Middle Eastern/North African (110 alleles). Whilst work has been done to ensure the databases are reflective of the allele frequency in the population at large, some statistical corrections are applied to the final frequency of an allele. A correction is applied to compensate for the possibility that within a local population some people might be more related to others than would be true for the population as a whole. The inclusion of a rare allele may overestimate its frequency of occurrence in the final statistic. Consequently, a size bias is applied to those alleles considered rare.

When the individual probabilities are multiplied together, we obtain the probability of two unrelated individuals having the same combination of alleles. For example, if four separate loci were considered (as was the case in 1994) and the respective probabilities of a particular allele at each locus were as follows:

Locus A – 1 / 10 (0/1)

Locus B – 1 /20 (0.05)

Locus C – 1/40 (0.025)

Locus D – 1/80 (0.0125)

The chance of two unrelated individuals having the same alleles at Locus points A, B, C and D is 1/10 x 1/20 x 1/40 x 1/80 = 1 / 640,000.

As the number of individual locus points compared has increased as technology has improved the concluding probability has got smaller. Or to put another way, the chances of a match being as a result of chance has reduced.

However, the probability of a false negative (that the match has occurred by chance) is only as good as the underlying statistical data which has been fed into the calculation (see further above). Each individual locus has an associated probability by reference to population specific databases, and assumes the Hardy-Weinberg principle holds true.

The Hardy-Weinberg principle states that the frequency of a particular allele within a population remains consistent over time, unless outside factors influence the population. The Hardy-Weinberg principle is influenced by the following factors: random mating (assuming no factors influence the choice of mate), large population size (or size of the sample from which probabilities are derived); no mutation (so no new alleles are formed and enter the population), no migration (so there is no interchange of genes with other populations), and no natural selection (so that no alleles have a particular reproductive advantage over others). As people with a different genetic make-up enters the general population through migration the frequency of a particular allele does not remain consistent. In those circumstances the particular odds of an allele featuring in the general population must be adapted to take into account potential deviations from the general principle.

A further limitation difficulty in calculating the probability of a random match occurs when low level DNA is detected. There may be an element of doubt over whether the peak is attributable to an individual or background noise. Further confusion is added where a mixed sample has been taken. Where three peaks occur at a particular point it is not possible to determine which peak can be attributed to which person. Therefore, the evidential significance of any point cannot be conclusively determined, albeit software has been developed to enable a statistical evaluation of complex mixtures with multiple contributors. A scientist may be able to say that a certain person could have contributed, or that there is no evidence that a person could have contributed.

The Prosecutor's Fallacy

A statistical based approach cannot definitively prove that the match did not occur by chance. There is always a finite chance of the match returning as positive when it is in fact false. It is therefore of great significance that those presenting forensic evidence do not overstate its evidential worth. This can be achieved by understanding what the statistic truly represents.

The match probability of a defendant's DNA or fibres to those found at a crime scene may be highly relevant to the relevance or strength of that evidence against him. As Phillips LJ remarked in *R v Doheny*[189]

[189] [1997] 1 Cr App R 369

It is easy, if one eschews rigorous analysis, to draw the following conclusion:

> 1. *Only one person in a million will have a DNA profile which matches that of the crime stain.*
>
> 2. *The defendant has a DNA profile which matches the crime stain.*
>
> 3. *Ergo there is a million to one probability that the defendant left the crime stain and is guilty of the crime.*

Such reasoning has been commended to juries in a number of cases by prosecuting counsel, by judges and sometimes by expert witnesses. It is fallacious and it has earned the title of "The Prosecutor's Fallacy".[190]

The Prosecutor's Fallacy is therefore a fault in statistical reasoning. Whilst named after prosecutors it is not specific to them and some variations of the fallacy can be used by defence lawyers arguing in respect of innocence. The reverse fallacy confuses the probability of finding the evidence on an innocent person with the probability that a person on whom the evidence is found is innocent. This is known as the Defence fallacy.

The fallacy has two separate elements for confusion:

1. The source probability error: because of the DNA match the DNA evidence establishes the suspected individual is the source of the crime stain, and

2. The ultimate issue error: because of the DNA match the DNA evidence establishes that the suspected individual is guilty of the offence.

The source probability error falsely equates the random match probability of DNA evidence with the probability of the accused being the source of the crime stain. The effect may be to falsely exaggerate the

[190] *Ibid* at 372

prosecution's case as it fails to consider factual information beyond the probability. Any conclusions on the source is inferred from the factual information surrounding the circumstances of the DNA placement and is ultimately to be determined by the trier of fact.

A good example of this is find in the *Doheny* appeal hearing, which quotes an exchange between prosecution Counsel and the forensic expert:

> *"Q. What is the combination, taking all those into account?*
>
> *A. Taking them all into account, I calculated the chance of finding all of those bands and the conventional blood groups to be about 1 in 40 million.*
>
> *Q. The likelihood of it being anybody other than Alan Doheny?*
>
> *A. Is about 1 in 40 million.*
>
> *Q. You deal habitually with these things, the jury have to say, of course, on the evidence, whether they are satisfied beyond doubt that it is he. You have done the analysis, are you sure that it is he?*
>
> *A. Yes."*[191]

The source probability error may be further compounded by incorrectly commenting on the probability of guilt. This is known as the ultimate issue error. As was noted in *Doheny*:

> *"Taking our example, the prosecutor's fallacy can be simply demonstrated. If one person in a million has a DNA profile which matches that obtained from the crime stain, then the suspect will be 1 of perhaps 26 men in the United Kingdom who share that characteristic. If no fact is known about the Defendant, other than that he was in the United Kingdom at the time of the crime the DNA*

[191] Ibid at 377

> *evidence tells us no more than that there is a statistical probability that he was the criminal of 1 in 26.*[192]

This example further provides a good example of the potential to fall into the Defence fallacy: it would be incorrect to say that there is a 25 in 26 chance of innocence. That approach would also fall foul of the ultimate issue error.

Common Limitations and Challenges on DNA Evidence

Whilst every case will be fact specific there are several factors practitioners will have in mind when considering the reliability of DNA evidence.

Timing and means of placing the sample: It is not possible to time when a DNA sample was left at the crime scene, or how the sample came to be placed at the scene. A suspected individual may have a legitimate reason for leaving their DNA at a crime scene. Further it is not possible to say how the sample came to be at the crime scene. This is particularly significant where an item could be considered a 'moveable item' – an item that can readily be moved from one place to another for entirely legitimate reasons.

Transfer of DNA: DNA can be transferred in a number of ways. Direct (primary) transfer occurs when cells are deposited directly on an object/surface directly from the individual whose cells they are. Secondary transfer (and to a lesser extent tertiary transfer) can also occur where an individual deposits cells containing DNA, which are picked up by another individual who then leaves them at the crime scene. Factors affecting the amount of cellular material transferred (and consequently the likelihood of secondary and tertiary transfer) include the individual's propensity to deposit cellular material (some people deposit more than others), the texture of the surface on which the initial deposit has taken place (a smooth surface is likely to retain less cellular material than a

[192] Ibid at 372

rough surface), and the amount of time and pressure involved in the contact.

Elimination samples: Where a mixed sample is obtained can profiles be identified from those that have had legitimate access to the sample during its chain of custody? Questions should be asked whether any results have been eliminated as a result of samples obtained from known individuals having legitimate access to the sample (in case of inadvertent contamination).

Human Error: Inevitably with any process involving interaction with human beings human error can arise. This could occur, for example, because of misinterpretation of the final charts, or inadvertent cross contamination or transfer.

The effect of a bone marrow transplant: It is worth enquiring whether, and if so when, your client has ever had a bone marrow transplant. The effect of a bone marrow transplant is to introduce the donor's DNA into your own which could affect any conclusions drawn by the expert witness particularly if a partial profile is found.

CHAPTER SIXTEEN

THE USE OF STATISTICS IN FORENSIC SCIENCE

Having considered the source of the forensic material its evidential significance must then be established. The role of a forensic expert does not end with establishing and interpreting the forensic material. What will often be key for practitioners is its significance, and how that significance falls within the context of the case. That is where the role of statistics can be used.

Some practitioners will have a background in mathematics and statistics, and so this material is more likely to come naturally. For others, less so. Practitioners should not be averse to asking for help and guidance in relation to complex matters of statistical analysis. An early opportunity for that to occur is to speak through matters with your own expert witness. Full and frank conversations over statistics (as well as expert evidence in general) can lead to greater effectiveness in cross examination, as the limitations of the statistical reasoning can be highlighted at an earlier stage. A follow up note following your conference with your expert can aide confirming your own understanding of the topic, as well as ensuring records are kept of what your expert has told you.

(Some) Key Statistical Concepts used in the Criminal Justice System

Bayesian Theorem: A form of statistical reasoning, that refines the likelihood ratio (see below) by using the likelihood ration multiplied by prior odds (the odds of something being the case before the introduction of new evidence) to develop posterior odds (the odds of something being true after the introduction of the new evidence).

Conditional Probability: The situation of determining the probability of an event after something else has happened (i.e. the probability of the second event happening is conditional on what happens first). For example, calculating the odds of the colour of the second ball pulled out of a bag is dependent upon the colour of the first ball pulled out of the same bag.

Defence Fallacy: The use of a probability value representing an evidential match, as argument that it represents the probability value of innocence.

False Negative / False Positive: An error in a measurement process that produces a false result. A false positive result is one in which a test gives a positive result which in reality should be negative. A false negative is the opposite. The rates of false positives and false negatives are a measure of reliability.

Independence: Where the probability of two events occurring have no effect on each other. For example, the probability of two heads having flipped an unbiased coin. The opposite of this is conditional probability (see above).

Likelihood Ratio: A measure of the value of the evidence, to help determine whether competing propositions are true.

Prosecutor's Fallacy: The confusion between the probability of finding evidence on an innocent person, with the probability that a person on whom the evidence is found is innocent. For example, confusing the probability of a match if the DNA came from another person is 1 in a billion, with the probability that the semen came from another person is one in a billion. The later statement is an example of the prosecutor's fallacy.

Random Match Probability: The probability of obtaining an evidential match within a population. This is not however the probability of obtaining 'another' match in the population having already obtained one match.

Random Match Probability

In relation to DNA evidence, another way of expressing the statistical significance of the evidence is by reference to the 'random match probability' or 'match probability' of the evidence.

The random match probability is the opposite of the likelihood ratio. It tells us the ratio between the likelihood that DNA belongs to the defendant compared to the likelihood that the DNA belongs to someone other than the defendant. In effect, the figure given tells us the probability that a person other than the suspect, upon random selection, would have the same DNA profile.

Where there is a DNA match based on a full DNA profile found at the scene of a crime, the match probability of 1 in a billion is often given. As outlined above in fact the real match probability is much more improbable.

Likelihood Ratio

In general terms, the likelihood ratio is expressed as:

> *"Probability of the observations (or evidence, E) given that a particular event (C) were true and given the truth of the background information), divided by the probability of the observations (E) given that the event were not true (C) and given the truth of the background information."*[193]

Applying that to a case involving the presence of fibres found at a crime scene, the likelihood ratio is the probability that the fibres found at the scene were the same as those from the jumper in D's flat, divided by the probability that the fibres were not from that particular jumper (assuming the truth of the fact that the jumper was found in D's flat, and any other relevant background information).

[193] As per *R. v T [2011] 1 Cr. App. R. 9*, para. 51.

In respect of DNA evidence, the likelihood ratio considers the following two probabilities:

P (E | PP): the probability in respect of the DNA evidence if the prosecution's proposition is true (that the DNA recovered is that of the defendant); and

p (E | DP): the probability in respect of the DNA evidence if the defence's proposition is true (that the DNA recovered is not that of the defendant).

The first probability gives the numerator of the likelihood ratio, and the second probability supplies the denominator. Therefore, if p (E | PP) = 0.1, and p (E | DP) = 0.01 the likelihood ratio would be 0.1/0.01 = 10.

A likelihood ratio greater than 1 supports the prosecution's proposition, whereas if it is smaller than 1 it supports the defence proposition. Where it is 1, it neither lends favour support to the Defence or Prosecution, and therefore is likely to be irrelevant and inadmissible.

A likelihood ratio may be expressed either in a verbal or numerical form. The following table outlining the equivalent verbal equivalent was outlined by the Court in *R v T*[194] :

Value of likelihood ratio	Verbal equivalent
>1–10	Weak or limited support
10–100	Moderate support
100–1000	Moderately strong support
1000–10,000	Strong support
10,000–1,000,000	Very strong support
>1,000,000	Extremely strong support

194 [2011] 1 Cr. App. R. 9 at para 31

Bayesian Theorem

The presentation of forensic evidence to a court involves both a prosecution and defence hypothesis. The prosecution hypothesis will link the suspect to the crime scene, whereas the defence hypothesis will suggest the suspect is not linked to the crime. When two competing propositions are presented a Bayesian approach to probability can be applied to the evaluation that considers the context. The context can be used to evaluate the strength of the forensic evidence, and can include a number of different factors including, how far the forensic material travelled, how long it has remained on the object, in what circumstances it remains on the object, or whether the underlying transfer can occur through an unrelated mechanism to the suggested transfer method. Bayesian theory therefore acts to refine the likelihood ration by considering the odds of something being the case before the introduction of the new evidence, to get the odds of something being the case in light of the new evidence.

Bayes theorem provides a methodology for forensic scientists to assess the evidential weight of scientific evidence, considering the background circumstances. It is therefore a form of conditional probability. In doing so it uses a likelihood ratio to provide this assessment.

In general terms, Bayes Theorem is expressed verbally as:

> *"Posterior odds (of an uncertain event, C) = Prior odds (of that uncertain event, C) multiplied by the likelihood ratio (provided by the evidence, E)."*[195]

Or mathematically:

$$P(A \mid B) = \frac{P(B \mid A) \times P(A)}{P(B)}$$

Where:

[195] As per *R. v T [2011] 1 Cr. App. R. 9*, para. 51.

P (A) = probability of event A occurring

P (B) = probability of event B occurring

P (A | B) = probability of event A occurring given event B has occurred

P (B | A) = probability of event B occurring, given event A has occurred

So, for example:

The likelihood that the jumper in D's flat is the same jumper that provided the fibres from the scene, taking into account the forensic analysis of the fibres = the likelihood that the jumper in D's flat is the same jumper that provided the fibres (not taking into account that forensic analysis) multiplied by the likelihood ratio (the probability that fibres found at the scene were the same as those from the jumper in D's flat, divided by the probability that the fibres were not from that particular jumper).

When will the court allow expert evidence providing a statistic to be adduced?

The general approach of the court was considered in the case of *R v T*[196]: The Court of Appeal considered Bayesian theorem and likelihood ratios in respect of footwear marks that had been recovered from the scene of a murder.

The expert in footwear marks concluded that there was a moderate degree of scientific evidence to support the view that trainers worn by the Appellant had made the marks. On appeal the use of this evidence was challenged as unreliable in substance. The higher Court held that in the area of footwear mark evidence it was not permissible to use the available data (as was available in 2010–2011) to calculate a likelihood ratio to reflect the degree of likelihood that marks were made by a particular

[196] [2011] 1 Cr. App. R 9

shoe[197]. This was on the basis that there was insufficient data on which an assessment could properly be made[198]. However, where there is a sufficiently reliable basis for calculation this form of evaluative opinion could be admitted.

Further the court outlined that an expert could use their own experience to express an evaluative opinion, in this case whether that mark could have been made by the particular footwear. However, that should not be in the form of a mathematical formula or ratio. That opinion should not be described as 'scientific'[199].

In respect of Bayesian theorem, it was noted that outside the field of DNA (and other areas where a firm statistical base existed) Bayes and likelihood ratios ought not be used.[200] It is worth emphasising that what was discouraged here is very specifically the Bayesian approach since the Court went on to approve the approach taken in *R. v Abadom.*[201] In *Abadom,* an expert used a government database to conclude that the glass found on the defendant's shoes and the broken glass at the scene of the crime both shared a refractive index which only 4% of glass in the database had. He then gave his opinion that this was very strong evidence that the glass on the shoes and the glass from the broken window were one and the same. Of significance for the Court of Appeal was that the expert did not refer to any mathematical formula. The distinction came down to a very simple and fundamental premise of evidence of an expert nature: where there was no sufficiently reliable evaluative basis for the admission of the evidence, it ought not be admitted.

Finally, the court reaffirmed an important principle: where an evaluative opinion is set out, the factors that enable an expert to draw that

---

[197] It was noted that the FSS database used contained 8122 shoes, whereas some 42 million were sold every year (at para 84).

[198] n.146 at para 85-86

[199] n.146 at para 96

[200] n.146 at para 90

[201] [1986] 73 Cr App R 48

conclusion, including any data relied upon, must be set out. The court, including all parties, must know how the conclusions have been drawn[202].

Several different types of expert evidence and their associated statistical evaluations beyond DNA evidence that have come before the courts.

Fibres: In *Simon John Hall v Regina,*[203] the expert for the prosecution, having found that the fibre samples from the defendant and the crime scene were "indistinguishable", was entitled to conclude that the chances of finding another (random) indistinguishable sample were "very small indeed." This conclusion could be drawn based on expertise alone and in the absence of any mathematical basis.

Secondary and Tertiary Transfer of DNA: The coding system of DNA allows scientists to calculate a probability of unrelated individuals having the same DNA profiles and the statistical likelihood of an individual being the donor of a profile from the crime scene. However, matters went further in *R v Reed and others,*[204] where expert evidence was given as to the possibility of secondary or tertiary transfer of DNA in relation to DNA found on a knife handle. On appeal, the Defence called two experts who stated that where the nature of the cellular material was unknown there did not exist sufficient research to enable an evaluation of whether that material has been transferred to the surface by primary or secondary transfer. The court concluded that, although the science of DNA transfer was incomplete, the underlying science was sufficiently comprehensive to allow the prosecution expert at trial to give an evaluation of the evidence using her experience where it was clear she was expressing her opinion as an evaluation of the possibilities without professing it in any manner that could be confused for scientific certainty.[205]

---

[202] N.146 at para 97

[203] [2011] EWCA Crim 4

[204] [2010] 1 Cr. App. R. 23

[205] *Ibid at para.* 126.

In *R. v Weller (Pet*er),[206] challenge was brought to the prosecution adducing evidence at trial of how DNA had been transferred. The victim in the case alleged that the defendant had inserted a finger into her vagina without her consent. A DNA sample was taken from the defendant's finger, which contained as a minor profile the complainant's DNA (the major profile being that of the defendant). It was agreed that there were five possible manners in which the DNA could have transferred to his finger. The prosecution expert asserted that there was strong scientific evidence to support the proposition that the DNA had been transferred by digital vaginal penetration. A defence expert instructed on appeal concluded that the evidence from an (as yet unpublished) academic paper was that the evidence actually went against this conclusion.[207] The Court relied instead on the expertise of the prosecution expert, finding this more persuasive. It found that the defence expert, as an academic, had no practical experience. Therefore, it was concluded, he could not fully challenge the logical cogency and clarity of the evidence of the prosecution expert.[208] The court concluded that it hoped that:

> *"the courts will not be troubled in future by attempts to rely on published work by people who have no practical experience in the field and therefore cannot contradict or bring any useful evidence to bear on issues that are not always contained in scientific journals."*[209]

This provides a striking example of the court's preference for practical, experiential expertise over an academic based approached to the evidence.

Firearm Discharge Residue ('FDR'): The statistical significance of FDR was given consideration in *R v George (Barry).*[210] It was alleged that Barry George had murdered Jill Dando by shooting her. During the investigation a single particle of FDR was recovered from the inside of

[206] [2010] EWCA Crim 1085

[207] *R. v Weller (Peter)* [2010] EWCA Crim 1085, para. 31.

[208] Ibid. at para. 38.

[209] Idem.

[210] [2007] EWCA Crim 2722

his coat pocket. During the course of the expert's analysis of this residue two opposing propositions had been formulated in respect of the evidence of the FDR in his coat pocket: that it supports the proposition 'Mr George was the man who shot Ms Dando', or; that it supports the proposition 'Mr George had nothing to do with the incident.'[211]

During evidence heard on appeal the experts considered that the chances of obtaining a single particle on the inside of a coat pocket supported both statements equally. In other words, a likelihood ratio of 1 was established. In those circumstances the evidence gave no support to either the prosecution or defence hypotheses. The court went on to allow the appeal, noting that the new evidence questioned the credibility of the evidence at the trial, and that the original evidence was a key part of the prosecution's case against Mr George. Consequently, the safety of the conviction was undermined. Mr George was subsequently acquitted at his retrial.

Footwear: In *R v T* [2011] 1 Cr. App. R. 9 the expert instructed at trial used the Bayesian approach in comparing the footprint left at the scene with a shoe found at the defendant's house. They found that there was an overall likelihood ratio of 100, concluding that the evidence provided moderate support for the proposition that the footprint came from the shoe found at the defendant's house. The Court of Appeal concluded that there was no sufficiently reliable basis upon which to reach this conclusion "based on the use of a mathematical formula."[212] This was on the basis that the database of shoes which the expert used to determine the rarity of aspects of the footprint was considered too small. The court did suggest that "If there was a sufficient database in footwear cases an expert might be able to express a view reached through a statistical calculation of the probability of the mark being made by the footwear,

[211] *R v George (Barry)* [2007] EWCA Crim 2722, para. 22.

[212] *R v T* [2011] 1 Cr. App. R. 9, para. 86.

very much in the same way as in the DNA cases subject to suitable qualification."[213]

Facial Mapping: The capacity of an expert on facial mapping to express an opinion as to the strength of identification evidence gained from facial mapping software has been approved in *R. v Atkins and Atkins,*[214] and *R. v Weighman.*[215] This is so even where there is no database against which to determine the likelihood that the matching features between the person recorded at the crime scene and the defendant could also match with a random third person/sample. In *R. v Atkins and Atkins*, expert evidence was given as to the extent to which facial mapping evidence supported identification on a sliding scale basis from "(0) lends no support" to "(5) Lends powerful support". Although there was no database against which to measure such assertions made in relation to two defendants (i.e. it could not be established how many others in the population would have shared the same features identified by facial mapping) the opinion was admissible so long as it was made clear to the jury that it was made in the absence of any database. It was noted that an expert who has studied this form of comparison can properly form a judgment as to the significance of the comparison. A judgment based on the expert's own experience (and nothing else) was sufficient, which the jury could then consider as part of its assessment. The absence of such evidence leaves the jury with no assistance to evaluate the similarities and dissimilarities of the comparison.

In Atkins, the Court of Appeal commented that they understood the anxiety surrounding new areas of expertise, and the courts should be scrupulous to ensure that evidence proffered as expert is indeed based upon demonstration of experience, knowledge or study. Self-certification, without demonstration, is insufficient[216].

---

[213] Ibid at para. 91.

[214] [2009] EWCA Crim 1876

[215] [2011] EWCA Crim 2826

[216] n.164 at 27

Can statistical analysis of forensic evidence alone be sufficient for a safe conviction?

As far back as 1997 in *R v Doheny,*[217] Phillips LJ mooted the possibility that

> *"the stage may be reached when a match will be so comprehensive that it will be possible to construct a DNA profile that is unique, and which proves the guilt of the defendant without any other evidence."*[218]

In the 23 years since passing that judgement science has continued to develop, and in turn the random match probability of DNA evidence continues to decrease. The courts have acknowledged that DNA evidence alone, where found in circumstances that call for an explanation, can be sufficient to found a conviction. As was noted in *R. v FNC*[219] the techniques of DNA analysis have improved markedly and what was insufficient evidence in years gone by will not necessarily be insufficient now.

The case of Jonathan Tsekiri[220] provides a good example. It considered the question of whether DNA evidence alone could be used to establish the guilt of an individual. Tsekiri was charged with robbery. It was alleged that the perpetrator of the crime had opened the driver's seat door where the victim had been sitting, assaulted her, before fleeing with an item of jewellery. Swabs had been taken from the handle of the car door, which came back showing the major contributor to the sample was the Defendant, alongside a minor contributor. The Defendant did not give evidence and was convicted, after the Recorder did not accede to a submission of no case to answer based on the sole evidence being the presence of Mr Tsekiri's DNA on the car door handle. On appeal it was argued that the DNA evidence alone was insufficient to convict, and that

---

[217] [1997] 1 Cr App R 369

[218] Ibid.

[219] [2015] EWCA Crim 1732

[220] [2017] 1 Cr. App. R. 32

the Recorder should have withdrawn the case from the jury at the end of the Crown's case.

The Court of Appeal disagreed. It was noted that in this case the DNA was left at the scene of a crime. That, without more was sufficient to raise a case to answer. The absence of an explanation would indicate there is nothing to undermine the conclusions to be drawn from the DNA evidence. The court noted that those circumstances 'can' raise a case to answer – in other words, matters are left on a case by case basis. Circumstance will inevitably play an important role[221]. As the court asked in Tsekiri:

> *"Is there any evidence of some explanation for the presence of the defendant's DNA on the item other than involvement in the crime? If a defendant in interview gives an apparently plausible account of the presence of his DNA profile, that might indicate that the prosecution had not raised a case to answer. On the other hand, the total absence of any explanation would leave the evidence of the defendant's DNA unexplained".*[222]

The interaction of the statistical/forensic evidence with other circumstantial matters surrounding that evidence is highly important: where a person is shown to be in the vicinity of the crime and to have matching DNA the chance of that being an accident may well be so low as for that evidence alone to be sufficient for the jury to safely find the defendant guilty of the crime; if the defendant in fact has a convincing alibi that can be supported in evidence prior to the close of the

[221] The court in Tsekiri considered the presence of DNA on an article associated with the offence, how readily moveable the article in question was, whether there was a geographical link between the defendant and the location of the DNA/offence, and whether secondary transfer could be a likely explanation as all relevant factors

[222] Tsekeri [2017] 1 Cr. App. R. 32 at para 15

prosecution's case, it may be improbable that they could be guilty of the crime and may give rise to a submission of no case to answer.[223]

[223] See *R v Doheny [1997] 1 Cr App R 369* at p.373.

CHAPTER SEVENTEEN

GENERAL TIPS WHEN USING EXPERT EVIDENCE

- Where possible, the identification of the need for an expert witness should be made as early as possible. This will allow the identification of the witness and funding arrangements to be put in place as early as possible during the life of the proceedings.

- Do not be afraid to ask colleagues and Counsel for advice on whether an expert witness should be utilised, and whether they can recommend a particular expert in a particular field.

- Have it clear in your mind what you want to achieve by using the expert evidence. This will ensure the expert instructed has the correct experience to be able to directly address the heart of the issue.

- Make it clear to the expert what you expect from them – a clear set of questions for the expert to directly address as opposed to a general request for assistance will ensure you get the focused responses you need. However, remember these questions may well appear in the final expert's report which will be disclosed if relied upon – be careful before disclosing any previously undisclosed admissions from your client!

- In advance of any conference with the expert ensure you have read the report and have some understanding of the science behind the expert's fields. Prior preparation prevents an ineffective conference.

- Your expert's time is just as valuable as your own – make the most of it. Ask the obvious questions where necessary. Ask about your client's chances at trial. Ask where the routes of cross examination are. The expert is an expert for a reason, and is an invaluable source of knowledge in preparing for your own role.

- Keep a note of the conference, and provide it to the expert immediately following the conference. Any errors in your own understanding, evidenced through the note, can be picked up on by the expert and corrected at an early stage, before they are highlighted during the course of the evidence.

- Ask your expert about their courtroom experience and take them through the process as far as is appropriate. Learning your expert has never been cross examined before during cross examination is not a positive experience.

- When defending seek disclosure of the underlying notes and workings of the prosecution expert – does the conclusion drawn in the final report feature in the underlying notes? If so, does it disclose further information about how they reached that conclusion than is in the final report? If not, ask yourself (and your own expert if possible) why not?

- Even the most complex of material can be broken down into a series of stages, allowing it to be understood. Having established your experts experience and qualification as an expert, lay the foundations of the expertise they are giving. Whilst you aren't going to turn your trier of fact from a layperson to an expert during the course of the experts witness a basic understanding of the expertise before going into the detail assists with the application to the particular case. Having laid the foundations, go into the detail before highlighting the conclusions drawn.

- When challenging an expert, only if you are sure you are right and the expert is wrong (or your instructions require you to), do not go head on with the expert's conclusions. Do not expect an expert to change their mind having drawn a conclusion. Tackling expert evidence is best achieved by either removing or shifting the foundations of their evidence. If it can be established that the underlying facts on which their opinion is based is wrong, the opinion can no longer hold good ground whilst allowing the expert to retain their credibility.

- Ensure the expert has taken into account all the relevant background information. If important information has not been considered this may result in a change of opinion, whilst allowing the expert to retain their credibility, as they had not been provided with the full facts.

MORE BOOKS BY LAW BRIEF PUBLISHING

A selection of our other titles available now:-

'A Practical Guide to Parental Alienation in Private and Public Law Children Cases' by Sam King QC & Frankie Shama

'Contested Heritage – Removing Art from Land and Historic Buildings' by Richard Harwood QC, Catherine Dobson, David Sawtell

'The Limits of Separate Legal Personality: When Those Running a Company Can Be Held Personally Liable for Losses Caused to Third Parties Outside of the Company' by Dr Mike Wilkinson

'A Practical Guide to Transgender Law' by Robin Moira White & Nicola Newbegin

'Artificial Intelligence – The Practical Legal Issues (2nd Edition)' by John Buyers

'A Practical Guide to Residential Freehold Conveyancing' by Lorraine Richardson

'A Practical Guide to Pensions on Divorce for Lawyers' by Bryan Scant

'A Practical Guide to Challenging Sham Marriage Allegations in Immigration Law' by Priya Solanki

'A Practical Guide to Legal Rights in Scotland' by Sarah-Jane Macdonald

'A Practical Guide to New Build Conveyancing' by Paul Sams & Rebecca East

'A Practical Guide to Defending Barristers in Disciplinary Cases' by Marc Beaumont

'A Practical Guide to Inherited Wealth on Divorce' by Hayley Trim

'A Practical Guide to Practice Direction 12J and Domestic Abuse in Private Law Children Proceedings' by Rebecca Cross & Malvika Jaganmohan

'A Practical Guide to Confiscation and Restraint' by Narita Bahra QC, John Carl Townsend, David Winch

'A Practical Guide to the Law of Forests in Scotland' by Philip Buchan

'A Practical Guide to Health and Medical Cases in Immigration Law' by Rebecca Chapman & Miranda Butler

'A Practical Guide to Bad Character Evidence for Criminal Practitioners by Aparna Rao

'A Practical Guide to Extradition Law post-Brexit' by Myles Grandison et al

'A Practical Guide to Hoarding and Mental Health for Housing Lawyers' by Rachel Coyle
'A Practical Guide to Psychiatric Claims in Personal Injury – 2nd Edition' by Liam Ryan
'Stephens on Contractual Indemnities' by Richard Stephens
'A Practical Guide to the EU Succession Regulation' by Richard Frimston
'A Practical Guide to Solicitor and Client Costs – 2nd Edition' by Robin Dunne
'Constructive Dismissal – Practice Pointers and Principles' by Benjimin Burgher
'A Practical Guide to Religion and Belief Discrimination Claims in the Workplace' by Kashif Ali
'A Practical Guide to the Law of Medical Treatment Decisions' by Ben Troke
'Fundamental Dishonesty and QOCS in Personal Injury Proceedings: Law and Practice' by Jake Rowley
'A Practical Guide to the Law in Relation to School Exclusions' by Charlotte Hadfield & Alice de Coverley
'A Practical Guide to Divorce for the Silver Separators' by Karin Walker
'The Right to be Forgotten – The Law and Practical Issues' by Melissa Stock
'A Practical Guide to Planning Law and Rights of Way in National Parks, the Broads and AONBs' by James Maurici QC, James Neill et al
'A Practical Guide to Election Law' by Tom Tabori
'A Practical Guide to the Law in Relation to Surrogacy' by Andrew Powell
'A Practical Guide to Claims Arising from Fatal Accidents – 2nd Edition' by James Patience
'A Practical Guide to the Ownership of Employee Inventions – From Entitlement to Compensation' by James Tumbridge & Ashley Roughton
'A Practical Guide to Asbestos Claims' by Jonathan Owen & Gareth McAloon
'A Practical Guide to Stamp Duty Land Tax in England and Northern Ireland' by Suzanne O'Hara
'A Practical Guide to the Law of Farming Partnerships' by Philip Whitcomb
'Covid-19, Homeworking and the Law – The Essential Guide to Employment and GDPR Issues' by Forbes Solicitors
'Covid-19 and Criminal Law – The Essential Guide' by Ramya Nagesh
'Covid-19 and Family Law in England and Wales – The Essential Guide' by Safda Mahmood

'A Practical Guide to the Law of Unlawful Eviction and Harassment – 2nd Edition' by Stephanie Lovegrove
'Covid-19, Brexit and the Law of Commercial Leases – The Essential Guide' by Mark Shelton
'A Practical Guide to Costs in Personal Injury Claims – 2nd Edition' by Matthew Hoe
'A Practical Guide to the General Data Protection Regulation (GDPR) – 2nd Edition' by Keith Markham
'Ellis on Credit Hire – Sixth Edition' by Aidan Ellis & Tim Kevan
'A Practical Guide to Working with Litigants in Person and McKenzie Friends in Family Cases' by Stuart Barlow
'Protecting Unregistered Brands: A Practical Guide to the Law of Passing Off' by Lorna Brazell
'A Practical Guide to Secondary Liability and Joint Enterprise Post-Jogee' by Joanne Cecil & James Mehigan
'A Practical Guide to the Pre-Action RTA Claims Protocol for Personal Injury Lawyers' by Antonia Ford
'A Practical Guide to Neighbour Disputes and the Law' by Alexander Walsh
'A Practical Guide to Forfeiture of Leases' by Mark Shelton
'A Practical Guide to Coercive Control for Legal Practitioners and Victims' by Rachel Horman
'A Practical Guide to Rights Over Airspace and Subsoil' by Daniel Gatty
'Tackling Disclosure in the Criminal Courts – A Practitioner's Guide' by Narita Bahra QC & Don Ramble
'A Practical Guide to the Law of Driverless Cars – Second Edition' by Alex Glassbrook, Emma Northey & Scarlett Milligan
'A Practical Guide to TOLATA Claims' by Greg Williams
'A Practical Guide to Elderly Law – 2nd Edition' by Justin Patten
'A Practical Guide to Responding to Housing Disrepair and Unfitness Claims' by Iain Wightwick
'A Practical Guide to the Construction and Rectification of Wills and Trust Instruments' by Edward Hewitt
'A Practical Guide to the Law of Bullying and Harassment in the Workplace' by Philip Hyland
'How to Be a Freelance Solicitor: A Practical Guide to the SRA-Regulated Freelance Solicitor Model' by Paul Bennett

'A Practical Guide to Prison Injury Claims' by Malcolm Johnson
'A Practical Guide to the Small Claims Track - 2nd Edition' by Dominic Bright
'A Practical Guide to Advising Clients at the Police Station' by Colin Stephen McKeown-Beaumont
'A Practical Guide to Antisocial Behaviour Injunctions' by Iain Wightwick
'Practical Mediation: A Guide for Mediators, Advocates, Advisers, Lawyers, and Students in Civil, Commercial, Business, Property, Workplace, and Employment Cases' by Jonathan Dingle with John Sephton
'The Mini-Pupillage Workbook' by David Boyle
'A Practical Guide to Crofting Law' by Brian Inkster
'A Practical Guide to Spousal Maintenance' by Liz Cowell
'A Practical Guide to the Law of Domain Names and Cybersquatting' by Andrew Clemson
'A Practical Guide to the Law of Gender Pay Gap Reporting' by Harini Iyengar
'A Practical Guide to the Rights of Grandparents in Children Proceedings' by Stuart Barlow
'NHS Whistleblowing and the Law' by Joseph England
'Employment Law and the Gig Economy' by Nigel Mackay & Annie Powell
'A Practical Guide to Noise Induced Hearing Loss (NIHL) Claims' by Andrew Mckie, Ian Skeate, Gareth McAloon
'An Introduction to Beauty Negligence Claims – A Practical Guide for the Personal Injury Practitioner' by Greg Almond
'Intercompany Agreements for Transfer Pricing Compliance' by Paul Sutton
'Zen and the Art of Mediation' by Martin Plowman
'A Practical Guide to the SRA Principles, Individual and Law Firm Codes of Conduct 2019 – What Every Law Firm Needs to Know' by Paul Bennett
'A Practical Guide to Adoption for Family Lawyers' by Graham Pegg
'A Practical Guide to Industrial Disease Claims' by Andrew Mckie & Ian Skeate
'A Practical Guide to Redundancy' by Philip Hyland
'A Practical Guide to Vicarious Liability' by Mariel Irvine
'A Practical Guide to Applications for Landlord's Consent and Variation of Leases' by Mark Shelton
'A Practical Guide to Relief from Sanctions Post-Mitchell and Denton' by Peter Causton

'A Practical Guide to Equity Release for Advisors' by Paul Sams
'A Practical Guide to Financial Services Claims' by Chris Hegarty
'The Law of Houses in Multiple Occupation: A Practical Guide to HMO Proceedings' by Julian Hunt
'Occupiers, Highways and Defective Premises Claims: A Practical Guide Post-Jackson – 2nd Edition' by Andrew Mckie
'A Practical Guide to Financial Ombudsman Service Claims' by Adam Temple & Robert Scrivenor
'A Practical Guide to Advising Schools on Employment Law' by Jonathan Holden
'A Practical Guide to Running Housing Disrepair and Cavity Wall Claims: 2nd Edition' by Andrew Mckie & Ian Skeate
'A Practical Guide to Holiday Sickness Claims – 2nd Edition' by Andrew Mckie & Ian Skeate
'Arguments and Tactics for Personal Injury and Clinical Negligence Claims' by Dorian Williams
'A Practical Guide to Drone Law' by Rufus Ballaster, Andrew Firman, Eleanor Clot
'A Practical Guide to Compliance for Personal Injury Firms Working With Claims Management Companies' by Paul Bennett
'RTA Allegations of Fraud in a Post-Jackson Era: The Handbook – 2nd Edition' by Andrew Mckie
'RTA Personal Injury Claims: A Practical Guide Post-Jackson' by Andrew Mckie
'On Experts: CPR35 for Lawyers and Experts' by David Boyle
'An Introduction to Personal Injury Law' by David Boyle

These books and more are available to order online direct from the publisher at www.lawbriefpublishing.com, where you can also read free sample chapters. For any queries, contact us on 0844 587 2383 or mail@lawbriefpublishing.com.

Our books are also usually in stock at www.amazon.co.uk with free next day delivery for Prime members, and at good legal bookshops such as Wildy & Sons.

We are regularly launching new books in our series of practical day-to-day practitioners' guides. Visit our website and join our free newsletter to be kept informed and to receive special offers, free chapters, etc.

You can also follow us on Twitter at www.twitter.com/lawbriefpub.